In the
of
this new day

In the gift of this new day

Praying with the Iona Community

Neil Paynter

wild goose publications  www.ionabooks.com

Contents of book © individual contributors
Compilation © 2015 Neil Paynter

First published 2015 by
Wild Goose Publications, Fourth Floor, Savoy House,
140 Sauchiehall Street, Glasgow G2 3DH, UK,
the publishing division of the Iona Community.
Scottish Charity No. SC003794. Limited Company Reg. No. SC096243.

ISBN 978-1-84952-447-6

Cover photograph © David Coleman

The publishers gratefully acknowledge the support of the Drummond Trust,
3 Pitt Terrace, Stirling FK8 2EY in producing this book.

All rights reserved. Apart from the circumstances described below relating to non-commercial use, no part of this publication may be reproduced in any form or by any means, including photocopying or any information storage or retrieval system, without written permission from the publisher.

Non-commercial use: The material in this book may be used non-commercially for worship and group work without written permission from the publisher.
If photocopies of sections are made, please make full acknowledgement of the source, and report usage to CLA or other copyright organisation.

Neil Paynter has asserted his right in accordance with the Copyright, Designs and Patents Act, 1988, to be identified as the author of this compilation and the individual contributors have asserted their right to be identified as authors of their contributions.

Overseas distribution
Australia: Willow Connection Pty Ltd, Unit 4A, 3–9 Kenneth Road, Manly Vale, NSW 2093
New Zealand: Pleroma, Higginson Street, Otane 4170, Central Hawkes Bay
Canada: Bayard Distribution, 10 Lower Spadina Ave., Suite 400, Toronto, Ontario M5V 2Z

Printed by Bell & Bain, Thornliebank, Glasgow

Contents

Introduction   15

First day
The ministry of the whole people of God …

    Thank you for the blessing of your call   20
    Let your Spirit whirl around us   21
    We are your people   21

Second day
The renewal of prayer and worship …

    Good gifts   24
    Our fondest thoughts of you   24
    Open to depth   25

Third day
Health and wholeness and the ministry of healing …

    A prayer for our wholeness   28
    A prayer for healing   29
    A prayer for the dark night   30

Fourth day
Church renewal; our local Christian community and new forms of being church …

    All of life is worship   32
    A prayer for setting off   33
    Being open for business   34

6   In the gift of this new day

Fifth day
Christian education and retreat centres ...

   Christ of the quiet places   38
   I am Mary and I am Martha   40
   Night prayer with blankets   42

Sixth day
The ecumenical movement; ecumenical organisations and bodies in our own countries and worldwide ...

   The long journey towards unity   44
   At the grassroots   45
   The Lord's Prayer   45

Seventh day
People of other faiths and beliefs; the promotion of understanding through dialogue and joint action for justice and peace ...

   Common heartbeat   48
   O Lord of the pilgrim way   49
   At the heart of creation   50

Eighth day
The implementation of the Community's economic witness; money to meet our needs and a just economic order ...

   Prayer for economic justice   52
   Help us to be accountable   53
   Prayer for money to meet our needs   54

Ninth day
People living in poverty; trade justice; aid and advocacy organisations ...

People living in poverty   56
Aid and advocacy organisations and movements   57
Trade justice   58

Tenth day
Those without access to education or training or employment ...

Prayer for mothers   62
In a time of austerity (from a demo for the end of Benefit sanctions)   63
God with us   64

Eleventh day
Young people, work with young people ...

My story: poverty, truth and dreams/prayer   68
Affirmation from Iona Youth Festival, 2015   73
Bless young and old in their living together   74

Twelfth day
Staff and volunteers on Iona and at Camas ...

Prayer for Camas staff   76
Storms and rainbows (an Iona prayer)   77
I have useful hands/prayer   78

Thirteenth day
The people of Iona and Mull, life in community ...

    Prayer of thanksgiving for Columba   82
    Prayer for the people of Mull and Iona   84
    God of the elements   85

Fourteenth day
The Word ...

    God of our words and wonderings   88
    Storyteller God   89
    We have need of ...   90

Fifteenth day
Those who sustain the world ...

    For their sustaining   92

Sixteenth day
Working groups, social action, working together for change ...

    Working together for change   96
    United in love, united in action   98
    Followers of the Way   99

Seventeenth day
Social and political action for justice, peace and the integrity of creation; victims and perpetrators of violence everywhere ...

This good earth   102
In your kingdom there are no warheads   103
You do not turn away   104

Eighteenth day
The United Nations (UN); implementation of the Millennium Development goals; UN Peacekeeping forces; peace movements and organisations everywhere ...

The United Nations   106
Peacekeeping, peace movements and organisations everywhere   107
Implementation of the Millennium Development goals   108

Nineteenth day
Human rights and gender justice ...

Dangerous Women Creed   112
Call us to your work   113
A prayer of confession
(from a service on Adomnán's *Law of the Innocents* in Iona Abbey)   114

Twentieth day
Racial justice and the rights of indigenous peoples ...

The road from Selma to Montgomery, and beyond
(on the 50th anniversary of the Selma to Montgomery march)   120
Your wandering people   121
God of all peoples, all communities   122

Twenty-first day
The environment and all who work for ecological sustainability ...

    Prayer of thanksgiving   126
    Prayer for a lighter carbon footprint   126
    In the gift of this new day   127

Twenty-second day
People without homes; displaced peoples; refugees and asylum seekers; our own commitment to hospitality ...

    Immigration/Home Office Prayers   130
    God of the exiles   131
    Into futures without fear   132

Twenty-third day
The renewal of community and the well-being of our own local communities ...

    Meditation and prayer   136
    In our local living   139
    A blessing for building community   140

Twenty-fourth day
Family groups; far-flung members; former members and associates ...

    The family of Jesus   142
    Gathered and scattered   143
    What it means to be family   144

Twenty-fifth day
Associate members and groups, friends ...

    Mantra   148
    Your will be done (A prayer from Church Action on Poverty)   149
    Prayer for stewardship   150

Twenty-sixth day
The growth and deepening of our life as an ecumenical Christian community ...

    Affirmation   154
    Embracing difference   156
    Resilience   158

Twenty-seventh day
New members; all whose lives have been touched by the Iona Community and for all we have received from them ...

    A blessing on a new member of the Iona Community   160
    All those whose lives have been touched by the Iona Community   161
    For all we have received from them   162

Twenty-eighth day
Intentional and basic Christian communities throughout the world ...

    The church born from below   164
    A vision statement   165
    The Corrymeela prayer for courage   167

Twenty-ninth day
Iona Community groups on the Continent ...

    A prayer from the Swiss Iona Group   170
    Gathered and scattered (prayer for a meeting by Skype)   171
    Together we are strong   171

Thirteenth day
Iona Community groups in the USA ...

    In a world which hungers for community   174
    A prayer from the Open Door Community in Atlanta, Georgia   175
    Scattered in so many places   179

Thirty-first day
On the thirty-first day of each month Iona Community members pray for members who have died

    Words to live by   182
    Prayer for travelling companions   183
    Prayer from the Iona Community's Hallowing Service   184

A prayer for the journey
'Who do you say I am?'   188

Sources and acknowledgements   191

About the contributors   192

Introduction

by Ian M Fraser

'The practice of the presence of God'

God chose not to stay aloof from the creation, but to come alongside human beings, inviting our cooperation in bringing the world's life to its fulfilment. That means for us something like becoming apprentices who look to the Master Craftsman for guidance, learning to hone native skills to play an increasingly mature part in shaping the life of the world in God's way. The Genesis stories of a) representative human beings, Adam and Eve, and b) the Tower of Babel indicate the disaster it could be for the world if human beings attempt to take over from God's final power. God, who sees the whole scene and can be turned to if we choose to do so, is at hand to guide and direct life.

The human race, time after time, let God down. Instead of going back to the drawing board to contrive creatures who were more amenable, God chose to come alongside in the Son, who accepted the terms of life as we have to live it, laying aside the glory of the Godhead, exposed to the rough and tumble of ordinary life as we are. Paul's second letter to the Philippians puts the situation Jesus accepted clearly: *'Though he was in the form of God, he did not consider equality in the Godhead to be something to trade on, but emptied himself, taking the form of a slave, being born as human as they make them.'* He lived a fully human life as God meant the human to be, not choosing any get-out when faced with crucifixion and death but seeing his assignment through to the end. Twelve legions of angels who could have been summoned to his rescue were confined to barracks. Thus God the Father at last had a humanity to work with, which came alongside us – *'in every respect has been tested as we are, yet without sin'* (Hebrews 4:15).

When Jesus Christ, resurrected, resumed his place in the Godhead, he made his mind and will available to us through the Holy Spirit; Paul urged that we *'put on Christ'*. The humanity which Christ exhibited is for us to adopt – not to obliterate our own beings, but to bring out our full potential in forwarding God's purpose.

Prayer, in the words of my mentor Professor John Baillie, is *'the practice of the presence of God'*: living with the awareness that God is at hand; making ourselves available, both as persons and communities, to be so conformed to the mind of Christ that we pray and work for God's kingdom to come and God's will to be done on earth as in heaven.

The 'practice of the presence' takes different forms for different people and at the same time can help integrate a community in its commitment.

A fellow member of the Iona Community once said to me that she could never give the time to daily prayer that I do. I replied that maybe what was asked of her was not in hours but minutes. Paul brilliantly describes the church as being like a Body under one Head, with different organs and limbs playing very different parts which fulfil different assignments contributing to the life of the whole. And the body sleeps! Once, on holiday, I could not get over a prevailing tiredness. It was as if God asked me how I started the day. I said, with some self-assurance, 'with prayers of the parish'. 'And you can't trust me to look after my own shop and give you a real break?'

I then realised we should have holidays from prayer!

Prayer may be so natural a part of life that it does not feature separately. Long ago I remember Richard Demarco speaking on TV about art. For him to be creative, prayer came in so naturally that it was as if it were mixed in with the paints he applied to the canvas. In Ecclesiasticus 38 the question is addressed: 'Who sustains the fabric of the world?' The answer is 'basic workers'. They carry the world forward from day to day. Others build on that (some pocketing as much as they can, at the expense of the essential wealth creators). The text goes on to note that prayer can be integrated into their work. It might be thought to be absent. But it is inherent. If my Margaret, so skilful with her hands, was knitting a jersey and a shaft of sunlight fell on it as it lay – showing up a tiny fault no one else would notice – the wool would be ripped back to that point and the part put right. I think of the Iona Community prayer *'we will not offer to God offerings which cost us nothing'*. To give one's best to a form of work which will bless humankind is, at the same time, a prayer-offering to God. On TV the night before I wrote this, a sea captain spoke about fishermen he knew: 'You will never find them in church – but their lives make it clear that they are people of faith and prayer.'

I became a member of the Iona Community in 1942 but was in touch from 1939. From the earliest days it was clear that we needed a prayer discipline to bind us, focusing on fellow members, the church and the world. What should be part of the Community's Rule remains open to challenge, but it essentially survives – though every new member has freedom to suggest changes.

When I was doing parish visitation in Rosyth, in Dollytown, an area of small houses, I knocked on a door.

A man opened it whom I immediately recognised to be a Communist shop steward prominent in the dockyard. Sharply he demanded, 'Why are you knocking on my door? I'm not one of yours.' I replied that I had been appointed as minister to the parish, not just the congregation. So it was in no way out of place for me to knock on his door. At the same time, it was the door of his house, and so he had every right to shut it in my face. We had a short exchange, and he did so.

I was doing a visitation in the area and knocked on the door again. This time we had a short conversation on the need for justice in dockyard, parish and country.

I was going to leave it at that. But at a later point people got hold of me: 'He's desperate to see you!' This time he pulled me into his house. His wife was ill and in hospital. She meant an awful lot to him. We talked about the deep springs in our beings which led us to revel in love for one another, especially those who were dearer than life itself.

He asked me then and there to pray for both of them.

I responded that I honoured his position and atheist commitment. I would not want him to feel pressured into what had no meaning for him, on the basis that we had discovered a natural human bond. He replied: 'Will you stop your bloody nonsense. Get down on your knees wi' me, and pray for my wife and mysel'.'

I stopped my bloody nonsense.

I knelt beside him.

Together we lifted his wife and himself in love to the God in whom he was not supposed to believe.

Prayer is not a religious activity.

It is a human resource.

Ian M. Fraser

First day

The ministry of the whole people of God …

Thank you for the blessing of your call

Thank you for calling us
to realise our potential.
Not be stuck in a false humility
that pretends we are not wonderful;
not minimising the beauty and diversity of the gifts
with which you bless us;
not pretending that we are worthless,
which is such an insult to you.

Help us to recognise just how wonderful we are –
and let us use our gifts to help others recognise theirs,
so that together
we can reflect your glory in serving and celebrating
and redeeming the world.

Zam Walker

Let your Spirit whirl around us

Unpredictable God,
forgive our staid, respectable hierarchies.
Our division of your labour into 'cans' and 'cannots'.

Let your Spirit whirl around us and through us,
abolishing the laity,
anointing all to offer all,
in the service of all.
Until all catch a glimpse of their worth.

David McNeish

We are your people

We are your people.
Together we make up your Body:
Your hands to reach out.
Your feet to walk with others.
Your arms to link in solidarity,
to embrace those who hurt,
to love and laugh and protest.

Enable us to realise that we are powerful beyond measure
because we together are your Body
and together can transform the world.

Zam Walker

Second day

The renewal of prayer and worship …

Good gifts

Gracious God,
you only give good gifts.
They are all fresh;
they come, minted with love,
from your soul of generosity.
Help us to reciprocate in kind:
to give you the worship of our hearts
with intention and affection,
as remote from dullness
as light is from darkness.

Wild Goose Resource Group

Our fondest thoughts of you

Wise and perceptive God,
humble us sufficiently so that from time to time
we let go our fondest thoughts of you;
for we need your Spirit to surprise us,
and she will never do that
if we always want to get what we like
and hear what is familiar.

Wild Goose Resource Group

Open to depth

Let us not turn the pages of holy scripture
as if we were skimming a novel.
You, the author,
are the God of depth and not shallowness.
So, enable us to find, among the words in your Word,
places where we can pause, reflect, wonder
and even disagree.
Then our faith will be lively;
then we will be listening for you
rather than reading the Bible.

Wild Goose Resource Group

Third day

Health and wholeness and the ministry of healing …

A prayer for our wholeness

God, who conceived us from the beginning of time,
who forms us, nurtures us, stretches and beautifies us;
to whom each life is of infinite value,
and in whom each life is cherished,
as you enfold us in your love,
may we enfold one another.

God, who gave us human form,
engineered our anatomy, and breathed into us life,
who warms our hearts with love, and fills our souls with the joy of living,
you gift us with intellect and compassion:
may we use our God-given gifts for the blessing of one another.

God, who promises to stay with us always,
you know us intimately and care for our needs;
when our bodies are frail, may we rest in your strength;
when hope seems distant, may we trust your word;
when loneliness stalks, may we know your presence;
when life feels too heavy, may we hold on to your truths;
and, when human words are lost to us,
may we hear your healing voice
speaking our name.
Amen

Elaine Gisbourne

A prayer for healing

Dear one,
I pray that you will be well;
that all which troubles you now will pass,
and you will be well.

Dear one,
I pray that many blessings come to you;
even in this moment,
may you be blessed.

Dear one,
I pray that healing will find you
through the blessings which surround you:
in the compassion of caregivers, in the skill of clinicians;
in the humour of friends, in the embrace of loved ones;
in the touch of a hand, in the strength of a prayer;
in the quiet of the night, in the warmth of the day;

and may God,
who heals and creates and re-creates,
bless you fully and richly
with love.

Elaine Gisbourne

A prayer for the dark night

When our future appears bleak, and the way ahead terrifies us;
when the night is dark and long, and our thoughts battle within us;
when we feel abandoned, afraid and believe we are alone,
Jesus says, *'I know, and I am with you.'*

When our bodies are wracked with pain, we cannot shift to ease,
our limbs stiff, joints on fire;
when distress threatens to overwhelm us, our spirits drowning in despair;
when the end of our life is close, and we dread the loss of our beloved ones,
Jesus says, *'I know, and I am with you.'*

Christ of Gethsemane and Golgotha,
you know what suffering is, and promise
that we do not suffer alone.

Christ of the opened tomb,
when the darkness threatens to overwhelm us,
may your Resurrection light be our hope,
that we may continue to walk our path with you,
beyond the valley of shadows
into the fullness of life which you bring.
Amen

Elaine Gisbourne

Fourth day

Church renewal; our local Christian community
and new forms of being church …

All of life is worship

Come, Holy Spirit,
renew the church for we are lost.
Lead us into a living tradition that does not fear change,
that repents of past wrongs and seeks to right them.
Teach us the language of today, not yesterday,
unglue our stuck practices
that we may be a living presence of the Gospel.

Come, Jesus Christ,
renew us, your church, for we are lost.
Lead us into the surprising edges of your kin-dom,
the places you inhabit so easily but we so often fear.
Show us how to live your values, not factional rules,
bind us as family
that we may reveal your heart in our lives together.

Come, Great Creator,
renew us, your creatures, for we are lost.
Lead us within the mysteries of all creation,
so – caught by wonder –
we may cherish the whole of it.
Help us to bring healing by our living, not more damage,
so all of life is worship
and our praise in church a just reflection of your glory.

Chris Polhill

A prayer for setting off

Transforming God – how can this be
that you call us
in the midst of our neighbourhoods.

In the knowledge of our precious story
and with all that is familiar around us,
you come with visions of new life.

Help us to be present to your Word,
to listen for need with a caring heart
and to be willing to trust in the hope
you have in us.

As we seek to follow in your Way,
help us to travel lightly
with all that seems impossible to us:
there being just a faithful few,
what feels to be a lack of resources
and the fear of the great unknown.

Hold us, Lord,
as we set off with little certainty of our destination.
Let us sense that you will reveal the bigger picture
in the fullness of time.

In this moment,
let us rest in the assurance that
one step at a time
is your way of faithful following.

'Then Mary said: *"Here am I, the servant of the Lord: let it be with me according to your word."'* (Luke 1:38)
Amen

Christine Jones

Being open for business

Reconciling God,
we come holding as precious
the gift of your story and all we have inherited.
In remembering together,
give us the wisdom to listen carefully
for those who have gone before us,
perhaps the people who brought us to faith:
what might shape their choices?

When our prayers reveal options
beyond our imagination,
help us to be careful with one another
in our different understandings.
Give us the courage to be open and honest in our discernment,
to care if divisions emerge,
to seek the views of the quiet ones,
and to actively listen to the strangers and neighbours
we are called to love.

Hold before us a vision for our time:
what might the Good News look like amidst
the poverty in our place;
where is the need for healing and release?

In opening ourselves for your business,
stay close, Holy Lord,
especially when fear threatens to become a stumbling block.

Liberate us as we look to the future
and dream of a legacy which echoes
your gift of unconditional love
for all humankind.
Amen

Christine Jones

Fifth day

Christian education and retreat centres …

Christ of the quiet places

This prayer was written for the 10th anniversary of Key House, which was a much-loved retreat place in Falkland, Scotland, run by Iona Community member Lynda Wright. This prayer celebrates the house, the table, the stable which was made into a chapel, the garden behind the house and the orchard and paths beyond.

Christ of the quiet places,
thank you for this place,
place of rest and restoration.

You do not offer bolt-holes or escape routes,
but space for healing,
time for preparation,
a safe house for recovery,
and shelter for the night,
along the way.

So meet us in the stable
as we pause awhile,
like wide-eyed shepherds,
before returning to the hills,
to the places of our work.

Sit with us at the table,
breaking bread with friends
before the testing time.

Come to us in the garden,
whispering our names
until we recognise you
and know ourselves again.

Walk with us through the orchard,
and along the gentle paths,
that tomorrow,
hurrying between the cars and through the crowds,
we may find you still beside us,
transforming urban landscapes with your gentleness.

But tonight, while we are here,
with all we have brought and all we have left behind,
and the outside door locked,
come and stand amongst us,
breathe your peace upon us,
unlock our fears, set loose our hopes,
calm us for sleeping,
free us for living.

Christ of the quiet places,
meet me in the hidden storms
and the silence of my soul.

Brian Woodcock

I am Mary and I am Martha

Read Luke 10:38–42, and then let God's Spirit pray through you …

Lord of earth and sky
as Martha did
I welcome you into the house of my heart;
as Mary did
I welcome you into the home of my thoughts.

> In service,
> in listening
> I welcome you.

Like Martha, I'm distracted:
so many calls on my time …
I run here and there
starting this and that,
never spending long enough,
giving people the impression
that I'm too busy for them.

Like Mary, I choose:
choose to slow down,
choose to sit at your feet,
choose to offer you
my ministry of listening.

Save me from feeling guilty
about the kitchens of the world:
the hot spots, the action areas
and help me to identify with your compassion
and your presence,
there as everywhere.

Welcomed and welcoming Christ
may all sisters come together
into your presence
and together eat at your table
the meal you have prepared for us,
that from the kitchen of your suffering
a banquet may be prepared
for all to eat.

Kate McIlhagga

Night prayer with blankets

Cradle us God
Fold us into your tears and laughter
Wrap us deep in love

Cradle us God
Weave us into truth and justice
Hem us round with hope

Cradle us God
Tumble us into questions and stories
Toss us up into joy

Cradle us God
Rock us into rest and dreaming
Cuddle us into your peace

Ruth Burgess

Sixth day

The ecumenical movement; ecumenical organisations and bodies in our own countries and worldwide ...

The long journey towards unity

Today, remember organisations that exist to help Christian denominations work together, among others:

Action of Churches Together in Scotland (ACTS) ...

Churches Together in Britain and Ireland (CTBI) ...

The Conference of European Churches (CEC) ...

The World Council of Churches (WCC) ...

Pray for the small professional staffs in each of these bodies
and for their committees,
as they try to create spaces
for ecumenical dialogue and cooperation.

At a time when all denominations are under pressure,
pray that Churches may resist the temptation to turn inward,
and that they find the strength and resources to continue
the long journey towards unity.
Amen

John Butterfield

At the grassroots

Pray for local ecumenism at the grassroots.
Remember the many small acts of kindness,
neighbourliness and hospitality
across ecclesiological and historical divides
involved in developing relationships between Churches.
However much Churches disagree over theology,
may we never fail to recognise our common humanity
and our common relationship
to the Lord Jesus Christ.
Amen

John Butterfield

The Lord's Prayer

The Lord's Prayer is the prayer of those
on their way to the Kingdom.

We pray it in solidarity with Jesus.

He gave his disciples the best he knew from his own experience.
At the deepest crises of his life
we find him using parts of this prayer.

When we use it we affirm, and enjoy, our solidarity with him,
crucified and reigning.

We pray it in solidarity with
every Christian through the ages.

All the saints now gathered before the throne
prayed it on their pilgrimage.

When we use it, we affirm, and enjoy, our solidarity with them.

We pray it in solidarity with
all Christians in the church throughout the world today:
all those who are facing their time of testing,
the great men and women of God whom we admire from afar,
the little ones whom we dare not despise.
This prayer is their resource.

When we use it, we affirm, and enjoy, our solidarity with them.

And we are challenged to pray it in solidarity with all humankind.
Their cry is for bread, for forgiveness, for deliverance.

We dare not use this prayer save in solidarity with them.
Thank you, Lord,
that as we seek to be in solidarity with them
we are not alone.
We have an advocate in your presence,
Jesus Christ your Son.
The saints triumphant pray for us.
We are upheld by the prayers of others round the world.

And so, as our Saviour Christ has taught us,
we are bold to say:

'Our Father …'

Jim Wilkie

Seventh day

People of other faiths and beliefs; the promotion of understanding through dialogue and joint action for justice and peace …

Common heartbeat

Lord of every person,
we remember today
those whose path to you is expressed
differently from our own.

We give thanks for our common heartbeat
and for the many wonderful ways in which
all of us can experience your presence in our daily living.

We think of the great range of faiths and beliefs in the world
and we thank you for the multiple routes which people take
in worship, prayer and discipleship.

May we always see in those of other faiths
pilgrim companions who, like us, carry your image
and are daily enfolded in your truth and hope.

Peter Millar

O Lord of the pilgrim way

Today we hold before you
the many people in our world who
through dialogue and awareness
are seeking to reach out to those who walk
within a faith tradition unlike their own.

At a time of many religious conflicts,
this is often a risk-filled encounter,
so we pray that dialogue,
whether local or global,
may be embedded in your wisdom and grace.

We ask that this work of solidarity
may be rooted in listening hearts
and approached with the kind of insightful patience
which is a marker of your relationship with others,
O Lord of the pilgrim way.

Peter Millar

At the heart of creation

God of the universe,
whose light shines in every culture and tradition,
hold close to you today the many women, men and children
who give of themselves in order to bring
justice and peace on this earth.

The bridge-builders, the artists, the hidden saints,
the risk-takers, the intercessors, the campaigners
and all those who will not lie down to injustice
even at the cost of their lives.

And may we ourselves be in their midst –
alive to the possibilities of your justice-filled Spirit
at the heart of creation.

Peter Millar

Eighth day

The implementation of the Community's economic witness;
money to meet our needs and a just economic order …

Prayer for economic justice

Down-to-earth Jesus,
you watched that poor widow put one small coin in the offering,
and you praised her generosity;
you knew why the tax collector was hiding in a tree,
and called Zacchaeus down to change his ways;
you told stories of economic oppression
and the struggle to make ends meet;
you talked more about money
than about spirituality or sex;
you taught us to pray for debts to be forgiven;
you announced the year of Jubilee:
'Here and now, this is coming true.'

Down-to-earth Jesus,
help us to get our hands dirty by being real
in our dealings with money,
in our campaigning for tax justice,
debt relief, a living wage, fair trade:
working for a new kind of economics
in the commonwealth of God's love –
here and now.
Amen

Jan Sutch Pickard

Help us to be accountable

On the back of an envelope,
on the back of all our busyness, baseline commitments,
budgets, blind-spots, impulse buying and anxieties –
O God, help us to be accountable.

For the money we earn, inherit, have saved,
the investments made in our name,
the security for which we've paid our stamp,
for benefits and bonuses, gifts and windfalls –
O God, help us to be accountable.

For the money we spend and what we hold back,
and the taxes we pay to keep society on track,
money shared with family; money given away
to strangers and good causes –
O God, help us to be accountable.

For the decisions we make, the clarity we lack,
the costs that we duck, the lifestyle we choose:
for our getting and spending, day after day,
and for the spirit in which we do all these –
O God, help us to be accountable.
Amen

Jan Sutch Pickard

Prayer for money to meet our needs

God of our daily bread,
we know that we cannot live by bread alone;
we know that money is not enough
for fullness of life.
Yet you know our Community, too:
our yearning to share the good news
through our programmes, through questioning and action;
you know our commitment to justice,
and the challenge to be good employers;
you know the way that we are charged
with stewardship of buildings.

Help us to recognise the resources we have,
to raise the funds we need most,
and to be clear about the priorities:

May we fulfil our calling with integrity.
Amen

Jan Sutch Pickard

Ninth day

People living in poverty; trade justice; aid and advocacy organisations …

People living in poverty

God of all life,
beyond our imagining, and yet coming so close;
you give the poor a place of dignity among the powerful.
You make a home for the homeless,
you refuse to leave those in need on the world's rubbish dump,
you see the greatness of the small.

God of grace and love,
we pray that no one may be threatened by hunger, malnutrition or scarcity.
Give bread to those who have none,
and hunger for justice to those who have bread.
Teach us what is enough for today,
and to share with those who have less than enough.
Let not the poorest pay for the welfare of the richest,
in unfair demands, benefit sanctions, excessive charges
and the cost of dodged taxes,
but let justice prevail.
May we live within your reality,
share your vision
and do your will
that the whole earth may echo your glory.
Amen

Kathy Galloway

Aid and advocacy organisations and movements

Creator God,
who sustains all, loves all, and has given the resources of the earth to all
and not just a few,
we give thanks for persistent people and movements everywhere:
small farmers feeding most of the world,
people setting up seed banks, maintaining biodiversity
and never giving up in the struggle for justice.
We are connected with seven billion people,
in a global community of trade, food, habitat.
Give us courage and faith to persist in solidarity.

Brother Christ,
who came to share our lives, to encourage and liberate us,
you live among us all.
We give thanks for dedicated people and movements everywhere,
challenging abuses of power, exposing corrupt practices,
defending human rights
and never giving up in the struggle for justice.
May we play our part in challenging greed and inequality,
creating more sustainable and equitable communities,
and treading more lightly on the earth.

Spirit of God,
who works among people and movements,
who moves our hearts and lives with love,
we give thanks for the people and places we care about.
And we pray for all who suffer anguish for the people and places they love,
for all whose livelihoods are threatened by a changing climate,
for all who work to improve the future for all our children.

May we join our voices in shouts of protest and songs of hope,
and never give up in the struggle for justice.

Holy Trinity,
whose promise is of a life
where all will flourish and be respected,
regardless of ethnicity, gender, sexuality or ability;
we pray that, as we live by your grace and sharing,
we may be led to make space for the voices of the voiceless
to be heard in the places of power
and compel our leaders and politicians to act for justice.

Kathy Galloway

Trade justice

Lord Jesus,
because you made great miracles of feeding and sharing
for people who were hungry,
so that everyone ate, and had enough,

so we pray for people everywhere without access to food
or the means to provide for their families;
for everyone denied their legal right to land,
for everyone facing harassment when they seek to make a living,
for everyone prevented from getting a fair price for their produce.

We pray for physical and legal protection
for those subject to unscrupulous practices,
for an end to the inequity and injustice of trade rules
skewed in favour of the most powerful
and the bias to the rich of those who write and implement the rules.

We pray for the people
who have seen their lives transformed by trade justice;
those now able to buy food and medicine,
send their children to school, access services;
the women empowered by economic independence,
forming producer collectives and trading co-operatives,
holding new hope for the future.

We pray for ourselves,
that we may be enabled to reduce our own complicity with trade injustice,
and may pray and work for the day when all trade will be just
and it will be exploitative trade which is labelled.
That all and not just some may enjoy the fruits of the earth.

Kathy Galloway

Tenth day

Those without access to education or training or employment …

Prayer for mothers*

We give thanks for the devotion of mothers to their children, and pray that all women may have access to a healthy diet before conception and during pregnancy.

We pray that governments act on scientific evidence showing that poor maternal nutrition and resulting low birth weight of babies adds to the risk of a lifetime of brain disorder in children, resulting in poor learning ability and school performance.

We give thanks for teachers struggling against the deprivation of young people, working to give them an education and preparing them for a lifetime contribution to the common good of their fellow citizens. And we pray for all children who have no schools to attend.

In the name of Jesus Christ.

Amen

Paul Nicolson

* *Information taken from* The Inequality of Health: Women Will Eliminate Poverty, *prepared by Professor Michael A. Crawford, Director, Institute of Brain Chemistry and Human Nutrition, London*

In a time of austerity
(from a demo for the end of Benefit sanctions)

We remember all who have died
while their income was sanctioned by a job centre;
who were overcome by any feelings of humiliation or shame,
by fear or distrust, insecurity or loneliness,
by a sense of being trapped and made powerless
under the abuses of power of the State
in a time of austerity.

In a time of austerity,
we pray in solidarity for the thousands of UK citizens
currently suffering sanctions,
which are imposed with the maximum use of the media
to blame decent people for their own unemployment and poverty;
for the millions of UK citizens
who are suffering under unmanageable debts due to high rents,
the Council Tax,
caps and cuts in social security,
imposed by Parliament.

We pray, too, for those in power,
that they may find:

the courage to work for and implement social and economic justice;

the will to build a 'well-being state' on the ashes of the welfare state,
in which rich and poor and Parliament
are in solidarity with each other;

the policies to ensure that no one will have to choose
between heating or eating,

the rent or the streets,
life or death,
due to the unjust enforcement of debts,
inadequate incomes,
or no incomes at all,
and sanctions.

In the name of Jesus Christ.
Amen

Paul Nicolson

God with us

We lament our society,
where changes to welfare budgets
and lack of employment or training opportunities
cause real poverty in our own neighbourhoods.

We are disgraced by the need to have food banks;
saddened by the lack of support for our young people
and the paucity of care for some of our elderly.

Where those without homes are dying on our streets,
and those who suffer from mental health disorders
are marginalised in their own communities,
we wonder where love lies.

On cold pavements,
through sleepless nights,
in the hunger and the fear
God with us …

We grieve for our world,
where wars separate families
and force them from their homes;
where floods wash away fertile soil and precious crops,
and drought drains life away;
where neighbour nations build walls
and throw weapons.
Where places of worship and public transport systems
are targets of terrorism,
we wonder where love lies.

When uprooted and displaced,
when injured and afraid,
in loss and in despair,
God with us ...

Lord of love and life,
whose very being is rooted deeply
in the soul of all your beloved,
may each of us be faithful in responding to your call:

bringing hope to those who despair,
bringing peace to those who know only conflict,
bringing healing, sharing joy
and being your love and life in the world.

God in us,
God around us,
God with us.
Amen

Elaine and Michael Gisbourne

Eleventh day

Young people, work with young people …

My story: poverty, truth and dreams

Georgina Shields is a Commissioner on the Poverty Truth Commission and a former volunteer on Iona and regular guest and leader at Camas. This talk was given at the launch of Monitoring Poverty and Social Exclusion in Scotland, *by the Joseph Rowntree Foundation …*

My name is Georgina Shields and I am 21 years old. My dream for a long time has been to get to university. It is something I've always wanted to do. I've seen other people do it. Other people who were brought up wealthier than me. People who have got money are expected to go to university. There's a stigma if you've grown up in poverty though. People like me aren't expected to go.

My community is quite hit hard with poverty. I live in Blackhill in Glasgow. There are problems with drugs and alcohol abuse and there's not much for young people to do. And although there's a park, it's full of needles, so there's not really anywhere for children to play either. The shops are takeaways, bookies, pubs and a corner shop, so there's nowhere to buy fresh food.

A lot of people in Blackhill try to keep it to themselves, but they don't have a lot of money and they are in poverty, but feel ashamed of the word, and a stigma about it. Quite often they put themselves in debt to be able to afford nice things so it doesn't show. But *I'm* not ashamed of where I come from. I'm not ashamed to say I come from poverty: because you shouldn't feel ashamed about it. It's just the way you are, it's the way your life has been.

Growing up was really hard because my mum's disabled and she's ill quite a lot. I became a young carer when I was about 13. My older siblings are way older than me and left home around about then. I had to cook and clean, and when my mum couldn't do something like shopping I had to do it. When I came home from school I had to practically be a parent, but to my mum. I had to do everything, and fit in my homework when I could. Money was really hard because my mum was on benefits. Sometimes she wasn't able to give me money for school and I had to go in and get my free lunch. I felt left out of the crowd … When I could take some money to school, it was exciting, to be able to go out with everyone else. I don't feel like *I* lost out on my childhood, 'cause my mum tried to make sure that didn't happen, but I did have to grow up fast. I don't feel I've missed out: I feel I've been given a life to be proud of. And it's got easier now. More people are able to help.

School was all right. It was hard because I got bullied, just for stupid wee things, but that made it hard. I liked learning, but the school didn't believe I could do all the levels I wanted to. They said they didn't want me to fail and thought I would, so they never let me try. I had done art and design and I loved it. I had got a 'B' in my intermediate two exam and I wanted to do higher, but the school said 'No'. When I asked why, they said my artwork was good enough but my writing wasn't. And though I asked, they weren't able to give me any extra support for my writing. I was always in the lower classes: that's just where the school expected me to be.

When I left school, I got involved with the GK Experience. GK is an organisation that works with children and young people in poverty in the lowest 10 per cent in Glasgow, and will take them on Residential and give them experiences they won't always get in the local community. They've helped me grow in confidence and helped me out along the way of being who I am and what I can be. They are practically my life. I've been a Young Leader with them now for about three or four years and I just became a 'blue hoodie': that means that you've grown in experience and you have a higher responsibility but less support. It makes me feel good because I've worked this hard to have something good out of it.

At the same time as getting involved with GK, I found out *I* had disability, which really hit me hard. I felt *so* low I couldn't do anything. I felt powerless. I was at college at the time, doing childcare. I didn't really want to do it, but the school were pushing people like me, and girls like me, into hairdressing or childcare. It was like they were the only options there were. I hated the course, and I got quite stressed out in the summer, knowing that I had to go back to college. I started volunteering for GK doing some office work, and really enjoyed it. At the same time, I looked up courses on administration and office work. I found a college that does late recruitment, and they took me on. I started an HNC, and I'm almost finished my HND now. I think if it wasn't for the GK Experience, I wouldn't have had the confidence to have gone for late recruitment and to change to the course that I wanted to do. And I wouldn't have applied to go to Iona as a volunteer for the summer either – somewhere I have always wanted to go. It was like the best eight weeks of my life. It made me grow up *so much*. And you ask anybody and they'll say: 'She's changed.' I went back at Christmas and have re-applied to go back this summer, 2015.

I knew about the Poverty Truth Commission. I knew they were looking for new Commissioners. I asked to join, because I felt that my points would be valid and I had a lot to say, because I live in poverty. It's a truthful organisation and it might make people *actually* listen. These are places that don't judge. They take you for who you are and they give you a sense of belonging. They are places I can go and be myself. Act like none of my life matters for that weekday or weekend. Knowing that I'm going to be back flung in is the shock, but that gives me strength to go through the hard stuff. There have been times when I have been so stressed out about everything that I've wanted to pack it all in – just leave, run away, but I haven't. I've stayed and I've worked through it. Money is really difficult because my bursary is based on what my mum gets, my mum's benefits, so I don't get a lot for my bursary, which means for me to be able to live for that month I have to take out a student loan.

I'm not a big night out person. But if I'm asked to go to a night out and don't have the money I don't go. And I'll happily say that to the person: 'I'm sorry, I can't come. I don't have the money.' And I can see them saying: 'Oh, but we'll pay, it doesn't matter.' But I'm like: 'It does matter: it matters to me.' Sometimes at college I'll go without eating, just because I want to save the money. A lot of people say: 'I never eat.' If you were with me for the whole day, you would see that I don't eat very much. It's hard for young people. There is so much pressure to wear the right brands. You feel so ashamed if you don't have the right stuff. Sometimes it even stops you from going to school. Some young people are labelled as 'hoodies' or 'rude' or 'disrespectful' but you have to give young people struggling with poverty a chance.

A lot of young people are being hurt and let down so much in their lives already, they don't want to let anyone get close in case they get hurt again. People need to open their eyes, and stop seeing us as statistics but as actual people. Then they may actually understand what life is like. People in my community aren't always seen as if they are going to get to university, or even do well in school. Our generation are changing it. It's opening people's eyes to see we're not all gangsters, we're not all toe-rags. We're actually human beings. And I still had my dream: my dream to go to university. Some people in my family didn't think that I would make it. They didn't think I was good enough, because I was from a poor area. But there have been people in my life who have believed in me: my big sister, people in GK, my friends, who knew I could do it. I just needed to believe in myself, which is a hard thing to do, to go against all the stigma.

When I found out I actually had a place in three universities, I cried. I cried because at this time last year I never thought I would be sitting here with three offers to go to university. I just can't keep the smile off my face – it's *so* good. And it just feels like life's falling into place. After the summer I'm going to be studying for a B.A. Honours Business Management at Glasgow Caledonian University. My dream is coming true and I'm living it right now. Thank you to the Poverty Truth Commission for encouraging me to speak today, and to all of you for listening.

Prayer

Pray:

– for young carers: for more money and help in the daily struggle ...

– for kids failed by the education system: for more support within school ...

– for all families living in poverty: for food, money and an end to stigma ...

– for all people being discriminated against because of a physical or mental challenge, or because of their religion or beliefs ...

– for The Poverty Truth Commission and all other groups and organisations 'working towards overcoming poverty and ensuring that those affected by decisions are central to decision-making' ...

– for people who are struggling to fulfil their dreams: pray that their dreams may one day come true ...

Georgina Shields

Affirmation from Iona Youth Festival 2015

The theme of Youth Festival 2015 was 'Welcome Home'. Participants – along with having a brilliant time on the pilgrimage and on a boat trip to Staffa to see the puffins – did work on the topic of immigrants and refugees, and on having a home and welcoming safe place to go to. At one point in the week young folk staged a peaceful protest around Iona, singing and carrying banners with messages such as 'Make a Change' and 'No One Is Illegal'. Following Youth Festival, folk took part in the 'Glasgow Sees Syria' vigil. This affirmation was composed by Youth Fest participants and read out in the Abbey during evening worship, which young people led …

Because God has shared his life with us, we believe that our lives are also made for sharing and so we will always look for ways to share our time, energy and possessions with others.

Because the Kingdom of God is a safe and welcoming place, we believe that everybody, regardless of gender, sexuality or race, deserves to have a home which is their safe place. And we will do our best to make this happen.

Because the voice of God is beautiful and creative, we believe it is wrong to use words that are harmful to others and so we will always use words that are kind and positive to build people up.

Because God has created a world of plenty, we believe that no one should be denied access to basic resources and that everyone has the right to ask for help when they need it: we will always be ready to help those who don't have what they need to flourish and will speak out on their behalf.

Because God loves and values everyone, we believe that nobody should be made to feel worthless and that everyone should feel at home in their own skin regardless of the shape or size of their own bodies. We will resist the pressure to conform to idealised 'norms' and accept and affirm each other as beautiful people.

Because Jesus confronted injustice, we believe that everyone has the right to raise their voice and take action whenever things need to be challenged and changed. So we commit ourselves to joining our voices and to helping and supporting each other in speaking out against what is wrong and in building a world which reflects the love, justice and joy of God's Kingdom.

Written by a group of 14-18-year-olds at Iona Youth Festival 2015

Bless young and old in their living together

Living God,
thank you for the energy of the young:
for their sense of fun,
their joy and zest for life,
their quick ability with technology.

Bless them in their anxieties,
their struggle to grow;
bless their questioning
and their search for truth.

Grant wisdom to those alongside them:
to laugh with and not at,
to take questions seriously,
to be a good model for living
and to encourage young people's gifts.

Bless young and old in their living together.

Chris Polhill

Twelfth day

Staff and volunteers on Iona and at Camas ...

(The Camas adventure centre, on the Isle of Mull, is run by a staff group with specialist skills, helped by volunteers. Young people from the city and elsewhere, and other groups too, come to Camas for a holiday and the experience of exploring issues, building relationships and facing new challenges through living and working together in community.) …

Prayer for Camas staff

We pray for the Camas staff,
giving thanks for their creativity and commitment,
love and laughter,
passion and patience,
and all their work and wisdom.

As, with open hearts and skilful hands,
they welcome young people and care for the centre,
may they *'grow in love, awareness and respect of self, others, God and the earth'.**

May all of us, wherever we live,
welcome the stranger,
hear your whisper in the trees,
see your beauty as the heron soars,
and honour all that you have created.

Rachel McCann, Camas Committee member and former Camas Coordinator and volunteer

* From the Camas Mission Statement

Storms and rainbows (an Iona prayer)

For work and worship
prayer and action
being and doing
for sharing stories and for sharing beauty beyond words
for long walks alone and for pilgrimages together
for the sound of the ferry and for the echo of church bells
for quiet time and for the wild dance of the Spirit
for storms that pass and for rainbows
for daffodils in bloom and for a night full of stars …

for all of these things and
for all of the ways these things
feed into each other,
for this life-giving food and
for the varied food of life,
for all of the ways you nourish us,
loving God – we praise you.
Amen

Neil Paynter, former volunteer and Resident Group member

I have useful hands/prayer

Poem by 2013 Work Week volunteers at Camas, taken from the blog the Camas Diary (adapted):

I have useful hands …

I drilled a hole
and moved some sand.
I lit a candle
and sewed some seams.

I sowed some lettuce and
baked some bread.

I made some soup
and I made a bridge.
I scrubbed a floor
then made some scones.

I drew a picture,
and painted a bed.

I have useful hands …

Prayer

Christ has no hands but our hands:
no hands but our hands
to do God's work in the world.

Christ has no lips but our lips:
no lips but our lips
to proclaim the good news.

Christ has no love but our love:
no love but our love to share
with the imprisoned, the silenced, the persecuted,
the oppressed, the marginalised.
Amen

Saint Teresa of Ávila (adapted)

Thirteenth day

The people of Iona and Mull; life in community …

Prayer of thanksgiving for Columba

Columba of
the rocks and roots and rolling waves,
of rain-drenched earth, changing skies and empty horizons,
of coming home and moving on.

Columba of
the music of wind and seabird cries,
the poetry of wild geese and lowing cattle,
the vision of sharing bread and stories.

Columba
man of solitude and simplicity,
community and compassion,
soul friend.
We celebrate with gratitude and hope
your being and your openness
to the blessedness of all things.

Columba who saw the blessing of beauty
and Iona as a light for all times,
with you
we weep
for depths of poverty
and pinnacles of wealth;
for hostility, impersonality,
suffering, indifference
and all that harms people
and all living things.

With you
we laugh
for humanity's raucous energy
and generosity of spirit;
for angels, smiling faces
and all that heals people.
We celebrate with gratitude and hope
your being and your openness
to the blessedness of all things.

Because of imagination, legend and prayer,
because of love and grace,
no act is inconsequential
and no story without significance.
In our knowing and unknowing;
in the quiet space held within
that is Columba's vision and forever Iona,
we hold memories, remembrance,
and the whisperings
of a people's pride.
We hold out for others
the poet's bread
and the people's poetry.

We celebrate with gratitude and hope
the holiness of being
and the blessedness of all things.
Amen

Joy Mead

Prayer for the people of Mull and Iona

We who live by land and sea,
by wide horizons,
clear sunsets
and stormy days;
we give thanks
for beauty,
for bog and mist,
mountain and heather,
for calf and cow,
ewe and lamb,
the bird on the wind,
the hearth and the song.

We are come from many places
through centuries of wrong,
of suffering, famine, loss.
We know of lives lost on the wave,
of lands lost to dearth,
and the cost of community.

We come before you,
established and stranger,
newcomer and settled,
youthful and aging,
lonely and loved.

Bless us all, keep us all, bring us all home
in the wonder of creation,
in joy and in struggle,

to neighbour, to traveller;
to serve without safety,
to linger in love,
in the paths of the saints.
Amen

Rosemary Power

God of the elements

God of the elements, Ancient of Days,
you gave us the land to feed and delight us.

Wind of the Spirit, bringer of growth,
you gave us each other to reach and restore us.

Jesus the carpenter, human in weakness,
you gave us our labour, to cherish your kingdom.

Bless us, restore us, stretch us to serve you;
Friend of all need, give us starlight to guide us,
on the road to your home with the people you love.

Rosemary Power

Fourteenth day

The Word …

God of our words and wonderings

God of our words and wonderings:

we are thankful for the diversity of language
and the rich potential of the words we use every day.
They are written on our bodies,
shaped in our hearts,
formed in our mouths.
Words have the power to express and shape who we are
and who we might become.
Through our use of words
and the images they create
we discover what it is to be human,
carrying within us the potential for
creativity or destruction,
gentleness or violence,
vulnerability or power.

Words can destroy any immunity we might develop
to human emotions.
As we attempt to creatively express our needs and longings,
may we use words with awareness and compassion,
respecting the needs and longings of others.

And when the moment comes when all has been said
that must be said
may we listen for the earth's heartbeat
and graciously embrace the silence.

Joy Mead

Storyteller God

Our hunger for stories is hunger for life itself.
We are thankful for the story-world of warnings, lessons,
wisdom and hope
which is within each one of us
and cannot be ruled or oppressed.
Each time a story is told
it is born again for the listener and the storyteller.
Help us to see that we are people of the one story
and the many stories,
the Word and the many words,
and that to understand our fellow creatures
we must hear the stories that hold not only their experiences
but their hopes, dreams, understandings and values.

A good story asks us to look
and see
and pay attention to things as they are …
and as they could be,
so the stories must be allowed
to go free and unpolluted.
Those who hold our stories hold our lives:
if we poison or corrupt the stories
we poison the people.
Help us to become people of lively imagination,
open hearts
and moral vision
who continually re-dream the world:
people with a story to live by.

God, the quivering Word in all creation,
we are thankful for the boundless nature of imagination
and the wonder of words.

Joy Mead

We have need of ...

Insight
to discover what is hidden,
to explore what lies below the surface,
to be receptive to the storied light,
to see how sharing our stories may develop
our sense of belonging.

Discernment
that we may know the good stories,
recognise the power of words to transform or poison,
to destroy or create.

Vision
to see that transformation begins with imagination,
that words can set us free and be seeds of hope.

May we have the wisdom to avoid cynicism and despair,
to use language positively and constructively;
to dance to life's rhythm in story, poetry and song.

Joy Mead

Fifteenth day

Those who sustain the world …

For their sustaining (Ecclesiasticus 38)

I

Lord God,
we give thanks for wealth creators, and pray:
for those who work on soil, water and air
to keep all created life sustained from day to day;
workers on farms, allotment-holders
and reservoir employees and air pollution inspectors;
for those who stack shelves and serve at checkouts;
for road builders and repairers and lorry drivers
who get supplies to where they are needed.
And for those who give enhanced quality to each day:
for parents and teachers, neighbourly neighbours,
bus drivers who keep families and communities together,
churches and faith groups,
those differently-abled,
whose need is met with understanding and compassion
adding to the resources humanity can show in loving responses.
We pray for their sustaining ...
In Jesus Christ's name.
Amen

II

We give thanks for examples of health-giving service, and pray:
for doctors, nurses, vets and auxiliaries;
for sewage workers;
for those who hospitably deal with immigrants, asylum seekers,
and those thought of as deviants from society's norms;

for those who wipe children's faces and tears away;
for those who restore electric cables and telephone wires in freezing weather;
for political activists who fight for a world of justice, truth and peace;
for charities which help to restore a full life to the injured and despairing;
for those who protect wetlands for birds and care for the environments
to make life for all good.
We pray for their sustaining ...
In Jesus Christ's name.
Amen

III

We give thanks for those who bear burdens, and pray:
for the bereaved, for single parents left to bring up children;
for rough sleepers bearing the burden of abandonment
by those who might give them refuge;
for those treated as unwanted, their being and gifts ignored or despised;
for young people who seem to face no worthwhile future;
for those harshly dealt with by landlords and self-serving companies;
for those treated as 'surplus to requirements' by society
and those who go alongside to share and care for them and lift spirits.
We pray for their sustaining ...
In Jesus Christ's name.
Amen

Ian M. Fraser

Sixteenth day

Working groups, social action, working together for change …

Working together for change

When you came among us, Jesus,
to announce the arrival
of God's new community
in the midst of our broken world,
you chose both words and action
to make your message plain.

And the model you left us
inspires us still.

For you chose to work
not on your own
but with colleagues:
men and women like us,
burdened with responsibilities,
often confused and anxious,
yet willing to be together
in your presence,
and slowly to become
the change that God still wants
for all peoples, everywhere.

So help us, we pray,
as we recommit ourselves
to working together for change,
with you,
in the place where we are –
for it is indeed holy ground.

Help us to look
with eyes of faith,
and see, not so much the weakness
or the failures
of our common action,
but rather the strength and the hope we have
through our different gifts
and our combined efforts.

And when people watch us,
no matter whether they admire
or criticise our actions,
may they be inspired by your Spirit
to stand up and stand together
in common endeavour
for the sake of the values
that you came to plant
among us.

We pray in your name. Amen

John Harvey

United in love, united in action

God, you have shown yourself
to humanity in many ways,
and we ask forgiveness
for any arrogance in us
which has sought to bind
your revelation
within our so partial understanding.

Yet we come to thank you
for that showing of yourself
in Jesus,
and all that he offers
in his Risen Life among us still.

Especially do we thank you
that you have shown us
your life as community:
one God,
Creator, Son and Spirit,
united in love,
united in action.

Forgive us for the ways
we so often fail
to mirror such unity;
for the times we have imagined ourselves
to be Messiahs,
rather than the ministers
we are really called to be.

You have set us
in communities
to work for change;
grant us the grace
to link arms with all
who share our hopes
and seek the good of all;
we pray in the name
of God in community,
Holy and One. Amen

John Harvey

Followers of the Way

When you chose
to come among us in Jesus,
you, God of all eternity,
chose a particular time
and a particular place.
So we remember today
the particular times and places
where the followers of Jesus
practise their discipleship.

Community halls, street corners,
shopfronts, living rooms,
pubs and clubs and churches,
each one a potential gathering place
for the followers of the Way.

We remember
movements and organisations,
local and national,
international too,
but each one grounded
in neighbourhoods and localities
and ordinary lives.
We give thanks
for secretaries and chairpersons,
for tea-makers and minute-takers,
and for all the host of helpers
who are your hands and feet,
living God.

On pavements, in parlours,
town hall and village hall,
we would celebrate, with the rich variety
of our communities of every
culture, generation, faith and sexuality,
the tapestry of our civic life
which enfolds and demonstrates
your life amongst us still.

As we work together for change,
may we ourselves become
the change you want us to be,
in the footsteps of him
who lived and died, and rose again,
that the whole of creation
might be made new.
We pray in Jesus' name. Amen

John Harvey

Seventeenth day

Social and political action for justice, peace and the integrity of creation; victims and perpetrators of violence everywhere ...

This good earth

Creator God,
we constantly affirm the truth
that the world belongs to you:
that in the beginning you affirmed your pleasure in creation;
you declared that it was good.
Our destiny is to enjoy the gift of this good earth;
our awesome task is to look after it for future generations.

Forgive our complicity in the pollution which threatens destruction;
forgive us that we do not always live up to the words we say
and the promises we make;
forgive us when we succumb to the paralysis of despair.

Bless and encourage those whose work and vocation it is
to preserve and conserve the earth's goodness.
Grant to us also the foolishness to believe
that we can make a difference,
in all the small things which,
though small,
can act and,
because they are convinced,
cannot be resisted.

Warren Bardsley

In your kingdom there are no warheads

Almighty God,
before whom all desires are known
and before whom there are no secrets,
we know now,
far better than our predecessors,
what we are capable of.
The skill and ingenuity of intelligent people can be harnessed
and bent towards violence and destruction.
We learned first how to crucify people,
and now we have learned how to crucify matter:
to destabilise the very atoms of existence and wreak havoc.
God, you know well how the fear of repetition
has governed so many decisions since,
become the nightmares
of so many generations of children.

And so we pray for peace.
For an end to the stockpiling and positioning,
the posturing and the flexing of nuclear muscle;
an end to the hypocrisy of hoarding
what we want others never to have.
Your prophet Isaiah longed for a time
when swords would be beaten into ploughshares.
We share that longing:
for all 17,000 nuclear warheads to be decommissioned,
regardless of their country of origin.
We pray for pathways to peace,
for ways that do not involve

threat and coercion, fear and intimidation.
We pray for the long hard pathway of peace
that is reconciliation, forgiveness and repentance.
In your Kingdom, Lord, there are no warheads.
Let your Kingdom come.

David McNeish

You do not turn away

Spirit of the living God,
we are often overwhelmed by the inhumanity of humanity
and the plight of so many victims of violence, war, torture,
trafficking, the exploitation of women and children …
and we can so easily turn away.

Remind us, then, that *you* do not turn away;
that you ache with compassion for both victims
and perpetrators of violence.
Save us from being intimidated
before the sheer size of the problem;
as we focus on one face … one family …
move us to empathy … in their pain to recognise him
who is both victim and liberator,
Jesus, our brother,
and discover that,
as we bring good news,
we ourselves receive and are changed.

Warren Bardsley

Eighteenth day

The United Nations (UN); implementation of the Millennium Development goals; UN Peacekeeping forces; peace movements and organisations everywhere …

The United Nations

God of all time and every place,
God of all peoples and nations,
whose loving purpose for this world is that all should prosper,
without fear, in harmony and mutual respect,
we acknowledge with shame that divisions, conflict and need abound:
the world is broken by the sins of our forebears
and by the continuing failure of governments to pursue policies and priorities
that lead to justice and peace for all.

We know that the United Nations is far from perfect:
it creaks, it is racked and hindered by petty politicking
and the hesitancy and reluctance of governments
to throw their whole weight behind it and fulfil their promises
to provide the necessary resources.
But it is still the best that we have as a means and opportunity
for achieving international cooperation.

And so we pray for the many-faceted work of the United Nations,
its staff and all its associated and related organisations –
far too many to name or remember in detail –
but we think especially,
in the context of our own concerns and priorities as a Community,
of the World Health Organisation,
the Commission on Human Rights,
the Intergovernmental Panel on Climate Change,
and the United Nations Relief and Works Agency
for Palestine Refugees in the Near East,
and UN peacekeepers in many different places …

May they all be blessed,
in your grace,
with wisdom, insight, courage and perseverance –
in Jesus' name.
Amen

Norman Shanks

Peacekeeping, peace movements and organisations everywhere

Living God, we pray for all peace-takers and peacemakers,
for all committed to sharing in the ministry of reconciliation,
for those engaged in conflict resolution and mediation,
for all peace movements and organisations
in every corner of the world.

We hold up before you the Fellowship of Reconciliation,
the Campaign for Nuclear Disarmament,
the Movement for the Abolition of War,
the Ecumenical Accompaniment Programme for Palestine and Israel,
Trident Ploughshares,
Scottish Christians Against Nuclear Arms
and other groups and projects with which our Community has strong links …

Even when the obstacles seem insuperable and prospects dark,
help us to remember that peace will be built by those who dream
and those who are patient, and that,
surprisingly, wonderfully,
even the smallest effort can contribute to the process.

Keep before us the vision of the perfect day
when all will be made new and nations and people
will live together peacefully and respectfully.
Through Jesus Christ. Amen

Norman Shanks

Implementation of the Millennium Development goals

God of justice and joy,
God on the move,
God in the midst,
we confess there is a long way to go
before these Millennium Development goals are reached.
We confess that we are complicit in the continuing failure of governments
to extend their horizons far enough beyond narrow national interests
and set their policies and priorities for the greater, higher good of all.
We know that these are lofty ambitions:
the eradication of extreme poverty and hunger;
universal primary education;
gender equality and the empowerment of women;
reduction of child mortality and improvement of maternal health;
combatting HIV/AIDS, malaria and other diseases such as Ebola;
environmental sustainability;
and the development of global partnerships.

But we also know and pray that,
with commitment,
with the sharing of skills, finance and other resources,
progress can be made.

And so,
as we remember all those who are suffering at this time
and all those who seek to help and support them,
we pray too, hopefully, and trusting in your grace,
for current discussions about additional specific
'sustainable development goals'
relating for instance to food security and sustainable agriculture,
climate change and access to water;
and we pray, longingly, ultimately,
for the transformation of the world,
that on the way to the building of your kingdom
political leaders and decision-makers may be blessed with
a breadth of vision,
with wisdom, boldness and compassion –
in Jesus' name.
Amen

Norman Shanks

Nineteenth day

Human rights and gender justice ...

Dangerous Women Creed

Dear God,
please make us dangerous women.
May we be women who acknowledge our power
to change, and grow, and be radically alive for God.
May we be healers of wounds and righters of wrongs.
May we weep with those who weep and
speak for those who cannot speak for themselves.
May we cherish children, embrace the elderly,
and empower the poor.
May we pray deeply and teach wisely.
May we be strong and gentle leaders.
May we sing songs of joy and talk down fear.
May we never hesitate to let passion push us,
conviction compel us, and righteous anger energise us.
May we strike fear into all that is unjust
and evil in the world.
May we dismantle abusive systems and
silence lies with truth.
May we shine like stars in a darkened generation.
May we overflow with goodness in the name of God
and by the power of Jesus.
And in that name and by that power,
may we change the world.
Dear God, please make us dangerous women.
Amen

Lynne Hybels, from member Rachel McCann

Call us to your work

God of all,
hear the cries of human beings everywhere –
for we are bound together by our common humanity;
hear the cries of those whose human rights are violated –
lives taken, liberties curtailed, personhood denied;
hear the cries of those who work for justice –
speaking out, taking action, valuing difference day by day.

Hear our cry
AND CALL US TO YOUR WORK.

God of the church,
you call your people to be a new human community –
showing your love for all across boundaries that divide;
you call us to stand up against injustice –
to work for a world where all can thrive;
you call us to be your people in all our variety –
in our relationships with one another and with you.

Call us to your work
AND HEAR OUR CRY.

God beyond gender,
hear the cries of our differently sexed bodies –
female, transgender, intersex and male;
hear the cries of our differently gendered society –
inequalities of violence, poverty and discrimination;
hear the cries of those who strive for transformation –
dignity, justice and flourishing for all.

Hear our cry
AND CALL US TO YOUR WORK.

God of all, God of the church, God beyond gender,
broaden our minds, deepen our commitment
and empower our action in your world.
AMEN

Elizabeth Wild

A prayer of confession
(from a service on Adomnán's *Law of the Innocents* in Iona Abbey)

In the year 697 AD the ninth Abbot of Iona, Adomnán mac Rónáin, devised and promulgated the Law of the Innocents. *Known as 'the first law in heaven and earth for the protection of women', the* Law of the Innocents *extended to children and clergy as well, and was enforced throughout Ireland, Scotland and Pictland. This law was an early attempt to limit the effects of war by protecting non-combatants, and it is the precursor of the Geneva Convention, the UN Declaration on Human Rights. It is an early sign in these islands of that fundamental Christian vocation to stand alongside the weak and vulnerable, to oppose injustice and oppression.*[1]

It is written that Adomnán did not carry a sword with him into battle, but the bell of Adomnán's Anger,[2] *which he rung out against the tyrants of the day,*[3] *and proclaimed against them:*

'My own wee true-judging bell
by which Irgalach is made childless,
I beg the true-judging King
that there may be no king from Irgalach …

The bell of truly miraculous Adomnán
has laid waste many kings.
Each one against whom it gives battle one thing awaits:
it has laid them waste.' [4]

Prayer:

Forgive us, God,
for times when we were deaf to the cries of the innocent,
when we had come upon injustice but
passed by on our journeys;
when we were unmoved
by the cries of children,
the tortured screams of women,
the cry of your beautiful and precious creation
being rent and broken and violated.

Forgive us for times when we were dumb,
when we did not sound out
because we believed you were deaf to our cries[5]
and to the cries of the poor.
When we took your silence for absence,[6]
when our tongues lolled in our mouths,[7]
or sounded excuses, reasons, rationalisations, empty promises.
Justifications instead of justice.

Forgive us our complacency,
and our complicity, God,
in this distantly divided but deeply interconnected world
where all actions and choices have their reverberations.

God, free us of all doubt and guilt and fear
and help us now to ring out:

To ring out in protest and praise,
in love and anger.
To strike[8] out against tyranny,
to sound out an alarm and wake up the world,
to announce Christ's good news of liberation and life,
to proclaim your justice until the Day of Judgement.[9]

Help us to summon our courage, God
and give us voices –
brave, clear and strong.

Voices that clang and disturb
create a stir
make waves
charge heavy, dead air,
touch hearts and souls with their passion and honesty.

Voices that clonk[10] and clank like the sound of hammers,
like the sound of hammers beating swords into ploughshares.
Voices that ring out and stubbornly keep on ringing out until

the whole of your creation is free from bondage,
everybody is fed,
all innocents are protected and held in respect …

O God, we have no power but the power that comes from you.
No strength but your strength.[11]
Come, fill us with your Holy Spirit
and hear our prayers as we call out to you
in our need and longing.[12]
Amen

Neil Paynter and Jane Bentley

Notes:

1. *Taken/drawn from Adomnán's* Law of the Innocents, Cáin Adomnáin: A seventh-century law for the protection of non-combatants, *translated with an introduction by Gilbert Márkus, Blackfriars Books, 1997.*

2. *'Adomnán did not carry a sword with him into battle, but the bell of Adomnán's Anger' – ibid. see p.11, paragraph 17.*

3. *In the article 'Ring Out Your Prayer: early Irish hand-bells', Spirituality magazine,* Spirituality 16, *January 1998, Gilbert Márkus writes: 'bells often appear in opposition to the power of kings'; and 'Such aggressively confrontational use of the bell is not unusual. The saint is portrayed defending his churches or his monks against aggression.'*

4. *From Adomnán's* Law of the Innocents, *p.12, paragraph 21, translated by Gilbert Márkus, Blackfriars Books, 1997.*

5. *The first three lines of this stanza were inspired by the R.S. Thomas poems 'No Truce with the Furies' and 'Counterpoint'. Poems quoted in 'At the Far Side of the Cross: The spirituality of R.S. Thomas', an unpublished lecture by Leslie Griffiths.*

6. *This line inspired by R.S. Thomas, and the lecture by Leslie Griffiths (ibid.). In the lecture Leslie Griffiths writes about D.Z. Phillips' book on R.S.Thomas subtitled* Poet of the Hidden God, *and discusses and quotes several R.S. Thomas poems which deal with the subject of God's absence and silence. Leslie Griffiths also mentions and quotes the philosopher Wittgenstein in relation to this.*

7. *This line taken from, or inspired by, the R.S. Thomas poem 'No Truce with the Furies': 'my tongue lolled, clapper of a disused bell'. Poem quoted in 'At the Far Side of the Cross: The spirituality of R.S.Thomas', by Leslie Griffiths.*

8. *'Strike' – See Adomnán's* Law of the Innocents, *translated by Gilbert Márkus, p.11, paragraph 18.*

9. *'Day of Judgement'– ibid. see p.17, paragraph 29.*

10. *In 'Ring Out Your Prayer: early Irish hand-bells', Spirituality magazine, Gilbert Márkus describes the 'clonking sound' of one of these 'prayer-machines'. He writes: 'That pathetic sound is the sound of real prayer.'*

11. *Ibid. Gilbert Márkus writes of the bell being rung in contemporary services by people 'whose help is in the name of the Lord rather than in their own strength'. He writes: 'To ring out ... is to enter into a tradition of prayer ... which seeks to transform the world not by getting power over it but by entrusting ourselves to God in prayer.'*

12. *'The sound of need and longing' – ibid.*

Twentieth day

Racial justice and the rights of indigenous peoples …

The road from Selma to Montgomery, and beyond
(on the 50th anniversary of the Selma to Montgomery march)

In the name of Jesus
the Cross-bearer,
we give thanks for those who trod that dangerous road in 1965
and laid down their lives in the face of violence and hatred
for the cause of justice for all American people:
Jimmie Lee Jackson of Alabama,
Viola Liuzzo of Detroit,
James Reeb of Washington …

In the name of Jesus
the Breaker of Barriers,
we give thanks for those diverse folk
who met on that same road half a century later:
Charlotte Rees, student activist from Colorado,
Corinne Crayton, colleague of Dr Martin Luther King,
Ray Hearne, peace campaigner from rural Tennessee …

In the name of Jesus
the Dauntless One,
we remember and pray for those who have given a lifetime of work
for full civil rights in America:
Ralph Worrell, veteran Trades Union leader,
Martin Luther King III,
Amelia Boynton, centenarian,
John Lewis, congressman …

In the name of Jesus
the Bearer of Faith,
we celebrate the courage, faith and cheerfulness of these

and many other sisters and brothers,
who challenge racism and injustice
whatever the cost,
who confront the powers-that-be
with the power of nonviolent resistance,
who heal the wounds of segregation
by an all-embracing love,
and who do not grow weary
in the cause of the Kingdom of God.
Amen

Iain Whyte

Your wandering people

How could we, your wandering people,
stray so far from you as to think we *own*
this small patch of land our ancestors settled?
If we plant and grow; plan and build,
why can't we look at what we have done and say:
'It is good. Let's share it'
and hear you saying: 'Yes, share it'?

If we send money (goats and worms and cows) to Africa –
that's good – of course.

But when Zimbabweans, or Syrians, or Somalis or other 'strangers'
(who are not *like us)*
come or flee here to *our* place –
we close the borders.
Build hellholes of prisons – Dungavel, Colnbrook ...

We give the keys and the freedom to shout, bully and terrorise
to untrained jobseekers,
themselves marginalised –
fear causing more fear:
a circle of terror.

God of Love,
where is love in all of this?
Where is generosity, hospitality, compassion?
Wake us up; challenge us.
Take us to the place of meeting and reaching out
and sharing and loving –
take us to the place of courage and action,
out beyond the fear and the meanness,
where we can learn from your hurting people the truth that
while anyone is in chains
none of us are free.

Isabel Whyte

God of all peoples, all communities

God of all peoples, all communities,
because we built ships and sought adventure,
we stole the land, the lives, the hopes of your people
and called it 'conquest'.
We stole their children, their communities, their future
and we called it 'empire'.

Yet now we acknowledge the harm that was done to so many people:
Aborigines, Native Americans, Maoris – so many.
And we did it in your name.

God of all peoples, all communities,
help us now to retrace our steps
along the 'rabbit-proof fences' we build
and pull down the walls of separation.
Make us humble, respectful listeners;
help us to be people who learn from the mistakes of history;
observers who see the risk of repeating the past;
builders who can rebuild;
lovers with open doors and open arms –
reaching out to repair the hurt
and embrace your people

Isabel Whyte

Twenty-first day

The environment and all who work for ecological sustainability …

Prayer of thanksgiving

Almighty God, Creator:
the morning is yours, rising into fullness.
The summer is yours, dipping into autumn.
Eternity is yours, dipping into time.
The vibrant grasses, the scent of flowers,
the lichen on the rocks, the tang of seaweed …
All are yours.
Gladly we live in this garden of your creating.

George MacLeod

Prayer for a lighter carbon footprint

Creator God,
we ask that you guide us:
empower us to understand the environmental experts,
who tell us that, by our wasteful actions,
we are in danger of destroying your precious world.
Enable each one of us to walk with a lighter carbon footprint,
by working out the best ways of living in this world of yours.
Help us to face up to the challenge of moving from old ways
to adopting new approaches:
keep us travelling along the Way with Jesus.
Amen

John Dale, Iona Community Carbon Coordinator, 2012-2015

In the gift of this new day

Creator God,

in the gift of this new day,
help me to notice the beauty
of all that is around me.

In the stillness of this new day,
help me to own my denial
of the effects of climate change.

In the business and busyness of this new day,
help my choices to be caring
for all life on earth.

Chris Polhill

Twenty-second day

People without homes; displaced peoples; refugees and asylum seekers; our own commitment to hospitality ...

Immigration/Home Office Prayers

It's easier to pray
for the ones made destitute by a faceless
decision-maker.

It's easier to pray
for the ones who disappear,
detained without time limit
at Her Majesty's Pleasure.

It's easier to pray for the
hunger-strikers,
their bodies wasting
in a protest of despair.

It's not easy to pray
for the one who
beckons the frightened
woman through the door
and laughs as he key-turns.

It's not easy to pray for you.
The one who stands before Parliament saying:
'Let them all drown if they
dare to cross
the Mediterranean Sea.'

It's not easy to pray for you,
the one who talks in a loud
voice behind me
on the bus, swearing

about anyone who is
not just like you.

God of the disappeared
Christ of the detained
Spirit to those who are hungering
for justice,

help me to pray faithfully, when stirred by pain.

God of unfathomable mercy
Christ incarnating forgiveness
Spirit answering cruel words with truth,

teach me to pray the harder prayers,
teach me of your mercy too.

Alison Swinfen

God of the exiles

So I will pray to you, God of the exiles.
Because our lesser gods of diplomacy have failed
and the gods of war rule and there are now
51 million refugees worldwide.

What do you want of us?

There are young men holed up
in Homs, in Yarmouk, besieged on every side.

What shall we do?

Your people
of the Cross, of the Book
kneel on the sands
and their throats are cut,
and their families
… their families …

What shall we do?

Did you hear me?

51 million.

Your people of the Cross, of the Book.

Should I cry out to you in statistics or in prose,
would you like an essay or argument,
poetry or a psalm?

Will we find a way through the horror
through the suffering
in numbers or in words?

Alison Swinfen

Into futures without fear

In the old days we learned
that you were not in the earthquake
and not in the storm
but in the stillness
in the breeze.

In the old days we learned
that you could use your breath and
all those lost, desiccated in the desert,
would rise, and return.

In the old days, they said
that those lost to the wilderness
were fed.

God of the stillness and breeze
God of the rising and the return
God of all absence and all plenty,

grant us the first lesson,
grant us that we may learn it again,
grant the faith that can look
upon the bones in desert
the bodies in the sea
and after the waves
of grief
and shame,

grant that we too may rise, turn again
and walk with our sisters and brothers
in your peace and into futures without fear.

Amen

Alison Swinfen

Twenty-third day

The renewal of community and the well-being of our own local communities …

Meditation and prayer

Lord, as we pray for the renewal of community
and the well-being of our local communities
help us to tease out what community means to us ...

Is it, perhaps, people gathered round a common task or purpose:
like-minded folk supporting each other through diversity,
or even to enjoy recreation,
or a physical sense of living within a specific location:
'my street', 'my town', 'my country'? ...

Is it a place where people go to experience 'living in community',
such as Iona, which people flock to in their thousands each year? ...

Is it a collection of people engaged in a common task at a workplace:
colleagues earning money to support their families,
or professionals linked by specific training? ...

Can we find it when we are with our friends in church,
when we pray together for the world,
or sing in a choir?
Is it perhaps in a gathering of Christians who share a Rule of life:
a shared commitment to justice and peace?

Or, do we find it within the group of family and friends
whom we love and support? ...

Lord, perhaps all of these are our communities,
and it is good to pray for them.
And so we take a moment to pray for them now ...

(Pause)

But what about those who live on the margins of our understanding;
those whom we do not know,
or even like,
or who speak a different language?

What about the young man
who sleeps rough in the doorway of the hall
in which the choir sings;
the young woman with needle-ravaged arms
who begs on the road outside the church;
the young people squatting in the nailed-up house
at the end of my road?

What about those I don't see or know about:
those alone, depressed, despairing;
the people across the world,
some dying of AIDS and Ebola;
and those who have a different faith or religion,
are they our communities?

Perhaps a better question would be:
'How can we build communities?'

Perhaps community is not a thing we can join, or live in,
set apart from others,
but rather an ongoing commitment to reach out in relationship;
even if that reaching out is to those we do not know,
do not like,
or do not understand.

Perhaps community
is not about feeling comfortable with like-minded people,

but more about embracing the challenge
of reaching out to others
in the world ...

Lord, as we pray for our local communities,
help us to listen to those around us:
to notice those with whom we share an affinity,
and those we do not,
and to rejoice in,
rather than fear,
our difference.

Help us to include
those who feel excluded
due to mental health challenges, disability,
poverty, gender, religion, age, race, sexuality ...

Help us to reach out and offer hospitality,
community,
to the unloved,
those on the margins of our world.

Help us to include those we would rather exclude,
embrace those we would rather disgrace
and learn from those we would prefer to forget.

Help us to listen,
rather than speak,
and enable us to embrace change
and not be fearful of difference.
Amen

Susan Dale

In our local living

In our local living
show us your will, Holy God.
Where to play our part
in our community;
where to give our energy and time;
that we may live by your agenda,
furthering the causes of your kin-dom.

Chris Polhill

A blessing for building community

May the blessing of the fierceness of God the Father
be in our actions,
as we strive for justice for those
who live on the margins
and who are excluded from our communities.

May the blessing of the compassion of God the Son
be in our hearts,
as we listen to the needs and wisdom of our neighbours,
in love,
with hope in our hearts.

May the blessing of the peace of God the Spirit,
who passes all understanding,
be in our minds;
may She rest on us, and in us,
and within our homes and communities,
as we reach out
to a hurting world.
Amen

Susan Dale

Twenty-fourth day

Family groups; far-flung members;
former members and associates …

The family of Jesus

Today we think about and pray for families ...

We think about the people Jesus considered to be his family –
not just his birth family,
but all those who gave up their lives
to follow his way.

We give thanks for those
who have given their lives in service
in the name of Jesus:
some at great cost to themselves;
others at the expense
of giving up material comforts and security;
others through following a path which
they might not have chosen ...

We pray for the strength and courage
to be prepared to make similar sacrifices
as members of Christ's worldwide family.
Amen

Katherine Rennie

Gathered and scattered

We give thanks for the family of Jesus –
those folk, linked together by his example and teaching,
who have committed their lives to following his Way.
We give thanks for this common thread of love and
commitment made by so many,
in whatever country, in whatever culture …

Today, we hold in our prayers members of families and
members of communities …

We think about the family that is the Iona Community,
folk linked together by a shared commitment to justice and peace.
We give thanks for the contribution each member makes
to further the pursuit of peace,
in whatever way,
for whatever good cause.

As a family, we pray together for peace in the world:
that people everywhere will be moved to play their part
in finding alternatives to intimidation, persecution and conflict.

Katherine Rennie

What it means to be family

On this day we pray for Iona Community members
past and present, near and far ...
We pray for this large family –
possessing all the attributes and foibles of many:
with times of love and togetherness,
times of bickering and estrangement:
times of pain and times of laughter.

We give thanks for the love and Spirit which binds us together:
a dispersed community united in its commitment to justice and peace.
We celebrate all that makes each of us different and unique,
yet part of the whole.

We pause for a moment to think of those in our family
who are suffering illness, sadness or loneliness ...
May they be upheld in arms of love and care.

We think about members of our family
we rarely see but pray for each month.
We give thanks that
although we are scattered across the country and across the world
we have the opportunity to gather regularly in Family Groups,
which enables us to share our concerns
in a setting of trust and understanding.
We give thanks for the opportunity to discuss and share more widely
at our annual gatherings and meetings
and at Community Weeks on Iona.

We give thanks for the support, encouragement, challenge and inspiration
that members can offer one another.

We pray that our family continues to play a meaningful role
within the world family.

As part of the universal family
we pray for peace in the world;
for those affected by violence and warfare.
May they feel supported in their plight
in the knowledge that others remember them
and are seeking alternatives
to conflict, persecution and intimidation.

We pray for all those who work for justice:
that through the Spirit
they may gain the strength and courage
to seek peace and pursue it.
Amen

Katherine Rennie

Twenty-fifth day

Associate members and groups, friends ...

Mantra

… as uttered in Darjeeling
by the old man from Sikkim
who turned his prayer wheel round
and round upon the axis of the world
with eyes of piercing mountain blue

These were his words
that sunny morning
thirty years ago
when I asked for
translation

Om mani padme hum
Om mani padme hum
Om mani padme …
Om mani padme …
God – come – to – my – heart

When the jewel of the mind – *mani*
rests in the lotus of the heart – *padme*
undivided – *hum*
Blessed are the pure of heart
for they shall see …
with eyes of piercing mountain blue

Alastair McIntosh, associate member in Scotland

Your will be done
(A prayer from Church Action on Poverty)

God of creation
we live in the world you have made
Give us generous hearts
to share your wealth with others
Your kingdom come
YOUR WILL BE DONE

God of power
help us to remember that you can do impossible things
Inspire us to work with you for change in our society
Your kingdom come
YOUR WILL BE DONE

God of hope
be present in our communities
Give us the strength to show your love right here
Your kingdom come
YOUR WILL BE DONE

God of love
you bring us healing and comfort
Come close to those who need your peace
Your kingdom come
YOUR WILL BE DONE

God of truth
draw us into your story of hope
Challenge us to speak out for justice
Your kingdom come
YOUR WILL BE DONE

Marie Pattison,
from associate member Niall Cooper,
Director of Church Action on Poverty

Prayer for stewardship

I call on You:
You who created the inconceivable and infinite cosmos,
because You also created our wonderful unique Earth.

I want to thank You, but I am ashamed:

Your world has become brutalised and laid to waste,
aspects distorted beyond recognition,
animals degraded to mere 'things' and exploited,
awe and reverence for life
destroyed by greed, excess and stupidity.

You, who rooted me in Your creation,
in this utterly beautiful planet Earth:
teach me responsibility for what I do:
eat, buy, claim for myself …

Teach me respect and reverence for life:
my neighbour: human, animal or tree.

Let me be gentle with the people around me:
with their fears and my own.

Help me to understand that we are all One:
that each of us has been called by name;
called to become aware and accept personal responsibility
for protecting and preserving our planet.

Will You show me the way? Help me? Daily?

Thank You. Amen

Marie-Helene Binggeli, associate member in Austria

Twenty-sixth day

The growth and deepening of our life
as an ecumenical Christian community …

Affirmation

For the joy of living together
  we give thanks.

In your three-in-oneness
you weave a pattern of joy,
   dancing between Creator, Son and Spirit,
   blurring the lines that divide,
   celebrating diversity in the unity,
   drawing us close:
   daring us to celebrate as one.

Your arms embrace all and each
and you say 'yes, beloved child'
to every particle of our
body physical, body
spiritual, body politic.

In the fragmentation of our individual lives,
   draw us, hold us,
   dare us to come closer to one another:
   close enough to catch the same breath,
   breathe the same air.

But we know that life together is not always easy.

In the struggles as we share
   breath and food
   homes and hearths,
   so close to the other,
   we pray for grace.

In the search for unity, as we share
   bread and wine
   space and place,
   so far from one another,
   we pray for a greater understanding
   of each other,
   and of your call to mission,
   that this call may be the
   pull, the draw, the dare
   that binds us
   to live, together,
   a countersign.
Amen

Ruth Harvey

Embracing difference

by Ruth Harvey

                                            Amen
                                  known in you.
                            of the Other made
                     and glorious uniqueness
               full-circle, in the utter delightful
            and reflected, as we come
        at the heart of our soul
each difference, nut-nestled

open always to embracing each pattern,
    new community, may we remain roundly
        leads to new relationships, new encounters
            As each round of prayer, each day
                right ordering, right time.
                    will restore us to your
                        unclear which pattern

>   Round we travel
>   through the month,
>   around the world,
>   embracing days and names
>   passions and pains, flesh and
>   blood in globe-spanning
>   corners and capitals.

>   Into each curve and groove
>   of our days you move, holding
>   out hope, as we hold on for
>   dear life to your hands and whirl
>   round and round sometimes
>   in circles, sometimes unsure
>   of where to go
> next,

Resilience

Dear Creator God,

when the rocks seem to move,
and the sand seems to shift,
when all around feels fluid,
I pray for the tenacity –
   to stay firm and open in faith;
   to embrace vulnerability as strength.

Dear loving Jesus,

when my soul feels eroded from the inside out
and the space between my inner self
and the self I share with the world
has become too wide,
I pray for resilience –
   for the courage to step deep,
   for the patience to restore my soul.

Dear Holy Spirit,

when in the midst of so many people
and so much diversity,
I forget my own belonging
and feel like a feather in the wind,
I pray for rootedness –
   for firm knowledge of your light that shines within,
   for trust that your wind will keep me safe and
   nudge me home to the sanctuary
   that is you.
Amen

Ruth Harvey

Twenty-seventh day

New members; all whose lives have been touched by the Iona Community and for all we have received from them …

A blessing on a new member of the Iona Community

May the grace of God shine on your face
May the justice of God encourage you
May the courage of God support you in the dark times
May the power of God keep you humble
and the humility of God inspire you
May the generosity of God surprise you
May the radiance of God dazzle you
May the faithfulness of God give you hope –
today and always.

Norman Shanks

All those whose lives have been touched by the Iona Community

Iona is a very thin place.
Glasgow is something else,
or is it?

God of beauty and wonder,
of prayer and politics,
we pray for all whose lives
have been blessed and turned around by you,
whether on the island of Iona
or on country roads or city streets.

Circle them with your grace and love.
Lead them into justice and wholeness.
Bless them always
and keep them close to you.
We pray in Jesus' name
and in the Spirit's joy and power.

Amen

Ruth Burgess

For all we have received from them

Thank you, God
for all who contribute
to the life of the Iona Community.

Thank you for people of all ages,
for travellers from around the world,
for pilgrims and friends and strangers.

Thank you for those who ask questions,
for those who listen to us and respect our stories,
for those who challenge conventions,
for those who draw us deep into justice and truth.

Meet us in each other, God.

Help us to be loving,
today and all the days of our lives.

Ruth Burgess

Twenty-eighth day

Intentional and basic Christian communities
throughout the world …

The church born from below

Holy Spirit of God who,
at Pentecost,
touched to new life a gathering of people,
male and female, young and old,
still we pray:
bring alive in our time communities who search
and find true ways of living for themselves and others.

In house churches and in small Christian communities,
as the church started,
may today the church born from below
encourage and sustain many in their pilgrimage through life,
giving light for the path they travel.
Thus may the shy be given confidence,
the weak be given strength through experience shared in community,
learning by *'speaking the truth in love to grow up in every way*
to the one who is the head, namely Christ' –
that the world may believe and find new life.

May members discover and bring into play
gifts which might have lain dormant,
contributing by prayer, worship and service
to the transformation of the world's life,
that God's kingdom may come
and God's will be done
on earth as in heaven.

May the life of 'simple church',
without pretensions or worldly clout,

keep before us remembrance
of Jesus Christ's command to disciples
that they take his way, a servant way –
promising that it is the humble, not the proud,
who will inherit the earth,
and that justice, truth and peace will prevail.
We ask it in his name.
Amen

Ian M. Fraser

A vision statement

I have been sharing this vision statement, based on words of Thomas Merton which I have adapted, with various church groups. It is a vision statement for any congregation regardless of denomination. It can form the basis of a challenging and encouraging discussion/reflection for any group seeking God's guidance. It is a vision statement attentive to the times in which we live and recognises that our worship and daily living are intimately connected.

– Peter Millar

- We believe that the role of any congregation is simply to seek God.

- We believe that God's people are called to be faithful in prayer, even in difficult times.

- We believe all of us are in need of forgiveness and healing.

- We believe that no one has a monopoly on truth: this belongs to God alone.

- We believe that God understands our doubts and our uncertainties.
- We seek to be open to those of other faiths and traditions.
- We seek a closer connection with the good earth, which often cries in pain.
- We seek to work for peace and for justice, locally and in the wider world.
- We believe that God is speaking to us in a special way through the poor and those on the margins.
- We know the value of both being active and sitting quietly.
- We seek to encourage people of all ages to be true to themselves and discover their inner gifts.
- We wish our leaders to be servants more than rulers.
- We pray that love will guide all our actions, and that our personal lives may know peace.
- We celebrate the beauty and wonder and mystery of each new day.

From Peter Millar

The Corrymeela prayer for courage

Courage comes from the heart
and we are always welcomed by God
the Croí of all being.

We bear witness to our faith
knowing that we are called to live lives of courage, love and reconciliation
in the ordinary and extraordinary moments of each day.

We bear witness, too,
to our failures and our complicity
in the fractures of our world.

May we be courageous today.
May we learn today.
May we love today.
Amen

Corrymeela Community

The Corrymeela Community is a dispersed community of people of all ages and Christian traditions who, individually and together, are committed to the healing of social, religious and political divisions in Northern Ireland and throughout the world: www.corrymeela.org

Twenty-ninth day

Iona Community groups on the Continent …

A prayer from the Swiss Iona Group

Dear God,
we thank you for life:
that you keep and sustain us every day,
that we have all we need
and more
and that we may live in peace of body and mind.

We thank you for the beauty of your creation:
for mountains and lakes,
and for the ingenuity of all those
who cared for this land
and worked for the well-being of its people.

We pray, God:
help us to be aware that our good life is not from our merit alone:
we are part of the web of the world;
help us to not harden our hearts
and close our doors
self-righteously
to the plight of so many poor people
all over the globe.

Help us to uphold the best of our traditions,
to be guardians of human rights,
to safeguard the dignity of the weak
and not fall back into narrow pride and
nationalist shortsightedness.

Help us to live together, not against each other,
because you are the God of all.
We praise you.

May all creation praise you!
Amen

Reinhild Traitler, a member of the Iona Community in Zurich

Gathered and scattered
(prayer for a meeting by Skype)

We meet by Skype on the 29th day of each month.
God, are you present among us?
Do you help us to care for one another,
to share what is important,
to become and live community?

I have my doubts – we are far away from each other.
I do not find means to really get involved by Skype.
Maybe I am too old to cope with these new ways of communication.

Let us find ways to pray together, to say a blessing.
Help us, God, to bring our spiritual needs into the Skype meeting
and share prayers to be connected to you and within the Family Group.
Then we might also find time for a weekend to meet.

Elisabeth Christa Miescher, a member of the Iona Community in Switzerland

Together we are strong

Good God,
give us the courage to stand up for justice and peace;
help us to be aware
that you hold us all in your hands.

Give us the strength of your Spirit,
Holy Ruach,
that She may empower us.

I am close to you all.
I heard the call to go forward on the path of justice,
not to accept injustice.
My influence is only small –
together we are strong.
Jesus, our friend and brother,
has shown us the way:
to keep our eyes open to discover signs of hope,
and to name situations of death and despair.

You, our God, called us to come to your House of Prayer
and to share our sorrows and longings.
You will help us to find means to change situations –

to open our borders to refugees and asylum seekers
and to share our bread and rice with hungry people,
our sisters and brothers.
God of peace and justice,
send your peace to our world –
we need it!

God, we thank you for the Iona Community,
where we are connected through prayer and action.

God bless us today
and on our walk together.

Elisabeth Christa Miescher

Thirtieth day

Iona Community groups in the USA …

In a world which hungers for community

Here, there is a mother struggling to feed her children;
there, we find a husband holding his wife's hand
on dementia's journey;

across town,
there is a crew re-habbing a home for a family;
on the other side of the world,
a kitchen is being remodelled for a young man in a wheelchair;

down the street,
two kids stand up to bullies at the school bus stop;
in an alley,
a nurse is bringing healing to a homeless vet;

in a 5-star restaurant,
the chef makes meals for 1200 hungry kids each night;
at the church,
folk bring in fresh produce for their neighbours
who have none;

in a parking lot,
people are packing to head out
to offer relief in a disaster;
at a food bank,
a teacher is gathering up donated supplies
for her students …

wherever we are,
whoever we are,
alone or together,
gathered or scattered,

let us serve as your Body
in the midst of a world which hungers
for community.
Amen

Thom M. Shuman, associate member in Ohio

A prayer from the Open Door Community in Atlanta, Georgia

Written for the 4th Annual Martin Luther King Holiday Human Rights Prayer Breakfast on January 12, 2007

Hungry are we,
O God of the oppressed,
for justice.

Thirsty are we, O God of liberation,
for human rights.

We come before you on this day-for-free,
O Creator,
that you are making.

In the midst of the empire's weapons
of mass distraction
we come

to focus
to commit
to act
to struggle
to fight

to love
to shout as loud as we can
to wage peace

for your abandoned ones
who wander the mean streets
with nowhere to go
in this nation at war
with Iraq and with itself.

You, Companion of Compassion,
who dearly love
beggars and prostitutes
children fighting rats under bridges
starving mothers whose milk cannot nourish
prisoners who sit in abandoned hellholes
without the visits that your son commands.

You who
come to us in the stranger's guise as
drunks and addicts
widows and orphans
beggars in velvet
mumblers and incoherent poets of your word of fire
teachers who dared to tell the way, the truth, the life
veterans who fought our wars abroad and have no homes in their homeland:
no security and no patriots' acts for them.

You, O God of justice,
you cry out
like a woman alone in childbirth:

'Housing is a human right.
Go tell it on the mountain
in the sanctuaries
on the streets
at the courthouse and in the halls of Congress:
House my people today.'

I say
in the fierce urgency of now:

Woe to you, prosperity preachers.
Woe to you, blind, cruel police
who hurt and harm my unhoused.

Woe to those who own two houses while I sleep in a barn.
Woe to the rich while I suffer from poverty.
Woe to the well-fed while I stand in the soup line.
Woe to those who cheer for tax cuts
while my people have nowhere to go but jail.

Help help help
us not simply to endure.
Grant us the strength to build the Beloved Community on earth,
to carry on with love and struggle and sacrifice in the streets.

Grant us dignity
as we build a destiny of righteousness and justice
of love and peace
of equality and housing for all
of human rights …

In the name of the one who lifted Dr Martin Luther King Jr
to be the brightest light of this nation
as he followed in the footpath of Jesus,
the Human One.

And as King confessed with his back against the wall:

'But amid all of this we have kept going with the faith that as we struggle, God struggles with us, and that the arc of the moral universe, although long, is bending toward justice.' (From 'Statement on Ending the Bus Boycott')

In the name of
Abraham and Sarah
Yahweh-Elohim
Allah
Jesus, the Human One

Harriett Tubman
Martin and Malcolm

Amen

Ed Loring, Open Door Community, Atlanta, Georgia

Open Door is a residential community in the Catholic Worker movement, which seeks to dismantle racism, sexism, heterosexism and violence, abolish the death penalty and war and proclaim the Beloved Community through loving relationships with some of the most neglected and outcast of God's children: the homeless and our sisters and brothers in prison.

Open Door members serve meals, provide showers and clean clothes, staff free medical and foot clinics, worship and share Eucharist together, and meet for the clarification of thought.

They have a prison ministry, including monthly trips for families to visit loved ones in various prisons in Georgia, and they advocate on behalf of the oppressed, homeless and prisoners through nonviolent protests, grassroots organising and the publication of their monthly newspaper, Hospitality. *The Open Door Community welcomes short- and long-term volunteers to join the work: http://opendoorcommunity.org. (Open Door is one of the Iona Community's sister communities.)*

Scattered in so many places

God in community,
who scatters yourself in creating, redeeming and sustaining,
hear our prayers for the work of our community:

into the silence surrounding oppression,
may we be a strong voice;

into the shadows of despair,
may we be the light of hope;

into the brokenness of lives,
may we be healing and strength;

into the emptiness of loneliness,
may we be a friend and family;

into the absence of faith,
may we be your face and heart.

Thom M. Shuman

Thirty-first day

On the thirty-first day of each month Iona Community members pray for members who have died

Words to live by

We name them one by one
in love and gratitude,
each recalled by us;
gently held by you.

We, too, are in your hands.
Your imagined ancient words
speak again:

*'I have called you by name;
you are mine.'*

Words for us to live by.
Words for those for whom we pray.
The gulf is not so wide;
you gently hold us all.

Amen

Brian Woodcock

Prayer for travelling companions

We recall them with prayers of gratitude –
travelling companions.

Those who walked with us,
sharing song and laughter
and tears and passion,
and faith and doubt and dreams.
Together we built community,
and tried to change the world,
praying, 'Your kingdom come.'

And those who walked ahead,
dreaming dreams, taking risks,
breaking new ground.

We recall them all.
They all walk ahead of us now,
on the next stage of the journey,
on a road still hidden to us.
They give us reason to keep going,
to honour them, keep faith with them.
They invite us to face what will be,
to embrace mystery
and be unafraid of that which we cannot know.

We recall them with prayers of gratitude:
they are not our past, but our future.

Brian Woodcock

Prayer from the Iona Community's Hallowing Service

Heaven is here, and earth,
and the space is thin between them.
Distance may divide,
but Christ's promise unites those bounded by time,
those blessed by eternity.
Let heaven be glad, let the whole earth cry glory.
Heaven is here, and earth,
and we are encompassed all around in the communion of saints …

For all the saints who live beyond us,
who challenge us to change the world with them –
we give thanks.
Christ be with them, Christ within them,
Christ behind them, Christ before them …
Especially we give thanks and pray for
those members of our Community far away:
encircle, embrace, encompass these we name now …

For all the saints who live beside us,
whose weaknesses and strengths
are woven with our own –
we give thanks.
Christ beneath them, Christ above them,

Christ in quiet, Christ in danger.
Encircle, embrace, encompass all members of our Community,
and also members of staff on Iona and Mull,
who offer hospitality and share the common life
with all who come …

For all the saints who went before us,
who have spoken to our hearts
and touched us with your fire –
we give thanks.
For the great company,
for Martin and Columba and Ninian
and Bridget and Hilda,
and for all the unnamed ones who are not forgotten
but held for all time in the memory of God,
and for our own most dearly beloved:
in the mystery of your love,
we are one with them now –
we give thanks …

Iona Community (adapted)

A prayer for the journey

'Who do you say I am?'

Lord Jesus,
you are a Lord who walks beside your people.
So we pray for people who march for justice.

You are a Lord who raises up those who are bent low.
So we pray for those held down by the grindings of life
and the indifference of the world.

You are a Lord who feeds the hungry.
So we pray for all who long for bread
and the means to provide it.

You are a Lord who celebrates the small and the insignificant.
So we pray for the children
and for those who are never noticed.

You are a Lord who says *'Follow me'*.
So we pray for courage, faith and cheerfulness in our hearts
that we may take up the cross and find it leads to life.
Amen

Kathy Galloway

Sources and acknowledgements

'I am Mary and I am Martha' – by Kate McIlhagga, from *The Green Heart of the Snowdrop*, Wild Goose Publications, 2004

'Night prayer with blankets' – by Ruth Burgess, from *A Book of Blessings*, Wild Goose Publications, 2004

'My story: poverty, truth and dreams, and prayer' – © Georgina Shields

'Prayer of thanksgiving for Columba' – by Joy Mead, from *Glimpsed in Passing*, Joy Mead, Wild Goose Publications, 2014

Dangerous Women Creed – © Lynne Hybels, from *Nice Girls Don't Change the World*, Zondervan, Lynne Hybels. Used by permission of Lynne Hybels

'A prayer of confession (from a service on Adomnán's *Law of the Innocents* in Iona Abbey)' – by Jane Bentley and Neil Paynter, from *Gathered and Scattered*, Neil Paynter (Ed.), Wild Goose Publications, 2007

'Prayer of thanksgiving' – George MacLeod, from *The Whole Earth Shall Cry Glory: Iona Prayers*, George MacLeod, Wild Goose Publications, new edition 2006

'Your will be done (A prayer from Church Action on Poverty)' – by Marie Pattison, used by permission of Church Action on Poverty and Marie Pattison

'A blessing on a new member of the Iona Community' – by Norman Shanks, from *A Book of Blessings*, Ruth Burgess, Wild Goose Publications, 2004

'The Corrymeela prayer for courage' – © Corrymeela Community, used with permission

'A prayer from the Open Door Community in Atlanta, Georgia' – © Ed Loring, from *Hospitality*, March 2007. Used by permission of Ed Loring

About the Contributors

Warren Bardsley: member of the Iona Community; formerly a minister in West Africa; worked for three months in East Jerusalem with the World Council of Churches Ecumenical Accompaniment Programme in Palestine/Israel; Convener of the Kairos Britain Forum and chairs the local Concern for Palestine Group in his home town of Lichfield.

Jane Bentley has been associated with the Iona Community for nearly twenty years since she first volunteered in the Community shop. She is now a member of the Community, and works in music in health and social care settings.

Marie-Helene Binggeli: Member of the Iona Continentals group in Austria, former biophysicist, now retired with a small garden and practising Sound Therapy. Engaged in various justice and peace concerns: children suffering from poverty and abuse, Amnesty International, Médecins Sans Frontières, the Clean Clothes Campaign, animal rights …

Ruth Burgess is a member of the Iona Community living in Dunblane. She is retired and enjoys growing fruit and flowers in her garden. Ruth writes and edits for Wild Goose Publications and Spill the Beans, an all-age worship resource.

John Butterfield is a minister in central Scotland. He is a member of the Iona Community, and during 2015-2017 is the Convener of Action of Churches Together in Scotland (ACTS).

Niall Cooper has been Director of Church Action on Poverty since 1997, and has been responsible for piloting a number of new approaches to anti-poverty work in the UK, drawing on international development experience, as well as running high-profile campaigns on poverty, debt and asylum-related issues.

John Dale: Solicitor, Anglican minister, Iona Community member, Iona Community

Carbon Coordinator, 2012-2015.

Susan Dale is a member of the Iona Community and works as a psychotherapist, narrative researcher and writer. She is committed to enabling others who are normally disempowered to develop a voice that is listened to. She is currently working on a collaborative narrative writing project in Machynlleth, where she set up and ran a therapeutic service to support the community following the murder of five-year-old April Jones.

Ian M. Fraser has been a pastor-labourer in heavy industry, a parish minister, Warden of Scottish Churches House, an Executive Secretary of the World Council of Churches, and Dean and Head of the Department of Mission at Selly Oak Colleges, Birmingham. He is the author of numerous books, including *Strange Fire, The Way Ahead: Grown-up Christians,* and *Reinventing Theology* (Wild Goose), which is used as a standard theological sourcebook throughout the world. Ian is one of the original members of the Iona Community who helped George MacLeod to rebuild the common life and the Abbey buildings on the isle of Iona. Throughout his life Ian has travelled the world, alone and with his wife, Margaret, visiting basic Christian communities. He has walked alongside slum dwellers in India and Haiti; Nicaraguan and Cuban revolutionaries; priests, nuns and catechists facing arrest and/or death in Central and South America; and small farming and fishing communities in the Philippines.

Kathy Galloway is an activist and writer, a member of the Iona Community, and currently the Head of Christian Aid Scotland. She lives in Glasgow.

Elaine Gisbourne is a member of the Iona Community living in Lancaster with her husband and three teenage daughters. She is a physiotherapist, working in a local hospice, as well as a Spiritual Director, Street Pastor and campaigner for world development issues. Elaine has a particular interest in healing and wholeness where there cannot be a cure, and when facing the end of one's life.

Michael Gisbourne has served as a parish priest for over 23 years and recently became Chaplain to the General Synod, facilitating the worship of that body. He is Chair of Lancaster Christian Aid and Chair of Praxis Northwest, and has been a member of the Iona Community since 2010.

John Harvey: 'I'm a long-term member of the Iona Community, based in Glasgow, and a retired minister, still seeking to rise to the challenge of our Community's commitment to justice, peace and the integrity of creation.'

Ruth Harvey is a writer, facilitator and mediator, who currently works for Place for Hope as Head of Training and Peacebuilding: www.placeforhope.org.uk. She has been a member of the Iona Community since 1993 and lived as part of the Resident Group on Iona as a child. She worships as a Quaker and is an ordained minister in the Church of Scotland. She lives in Cumbria with her family.

Lynne Hybels is an author and advocate for global engagement. In 2009 she started a fundraising campaign for victims of war in the Democratic Republic of Congo, and is currently raising funds and awareness for Syrian and Iraqi refugees. Lynne hosts educational tours in the Holy Land focused on reconciliation efforts between Israelis and Palestinians. In 1975, Lynne and her husband, Bill, started Willow Creek Community Church.

Christine Jones is an Iona Community member and Methodist minister. The church and community prayers here emerged from a journey with a town-centre church where a traditional Victorian building was transformed to embrace a community café within a worship area. A small, elderly congregation travelled faithfully with the need to dream, make sacrificial decisions and let go of much that was familiar, all the time asking what it meant for a church to be 'open for business'.

Ed Loring is a founder of the Open Door Community in Atlanta, Georgia.

George MacLeod, who died in 1991, is the Founder of the Iona Community.

Rachel McCann is a gardener, activist and former social worker, who lived and worked alongside people in poverty for many years.

Kate McIlhagga was a minister and a member of the Iona Community until her death in 2002.

Alastair McIntosh is the Quaker representative on the Iona Community (advisory) Board, and the author of books, including *Soil and Soul* (Aurum Press) and *Spiritual Activism* (Green Books).

David McNeish is a minister and singer/songwriter living and working in the West Mainland of Orkney. Prior to ministry, David worked as a campaigner for the CAB service, a worship musician and a hospital doctor, though not all at the same time. He is a member of the Iona Community.

Joy Mead is a poet, member of the Iona Community and author of many books, including *The One Loaf, Making Peace in Practice and Poetry, Where Are the Altars?,* and *Glimpsed in Passing* (Wild Goose Publications).

Elisabeth Christa Miescher was an Ecumenical Accompanier in Palestine in 2007, and is a member of the Iona Community.

Peter Millar is a member of the Iona Community, a soul friend to many and an activist and writer.

Paul Nicolson was ordained as a worker priest in the Church of England in 1968. He spent 16 years in the parochial ministry, during which time he founded the Zacchaeus 2000 Trust to work with impoverished debtors tangled in the UK benefit system. Wanting to escape the restrictions on campaigning against poverty imposed by the Charity Commission, he founded Taxpayers Against Poverty as a not-for-profit company in 2012. The prayer for those who died after a benefit sanction stopped their income was first said at a demonstration by the UNITE Community in 2014 outside the DWP headquarters in Tothill Street, Westminster.

Marie Pattison is director of Katherine House, a retreat house in Salford owned by the Faithful Companions of Jesus. She has worked for the Student Christian Movement and for the British Jesuits with young people volunteering in marginalised communities. Believing that faith and justice go hand in hand, she has campaigned with Church Action on Poverty for a number of years.

Neil Paynter is an editor, writer and late-night piano player, who lives with his partner Helen, his mum and Stevie the cat in a flat in Biggar, Scotland. He is the author of *Down to Earth: Stories and Sketches* (Wild Goose Publications).

Chris Polhill is a member of the Iona Community and one of the first women to be ordained a priest in the Church of England. She longs for the healing of the planet and for the kind of equality that realises people's giftedness regardless of who they are.

Rosemary Power is a member of the Iona Community who works in spirituality and justice issues, currently conflict within the Christian tradition. She has written books and articles on the prayers and traditions of Ireland and Gaelic Scotland, and on pilgrimage.

Katherine Rennie is a retired solicitor who specialised in family and mental health matters; she was also a family mediator. She is a local preacher for the Methodist Church in Strathclyde and is secretary to the Board of Trustees for a Night shelter for asylum seekers in Glasgow.

Norman Shanks is a retired Church of Scotland minister and a member and former Leader of the Iona Community. For eight years he was a member of the Central Committee of the World Council of Churches and is currently a non-executive director of the Greater Glasgow and Clyde Health Board.

Georgina Shields is a Commissioner on the Poverty Truth Commission and has recently started university.

About the contributors

Thom M. Shuman is a semi-retired pastor doing transitional ministry in Columbus, Ohio. He is strongly supportive of persons with developmental disabilities, committed to justice for immigrants and refugees, and a lifelong believer in nonviolence. He is an associate of the Iona Community.

Jan Sutch Pickard: 'I wonder whether it is high-mindedness or laziness that makes me say 'it's only money'? Years as a single head of household, then being a staff member in the Iona Community's island centres, then being a volunteer with EAPPI, living in Palestinian villages, meant that I learned to cope on a low income – needing to know the price of a loaf of bread – and to value living simply. Also, being bad at maths, I didn't try to understand economics! However, the Iona Community's Economic Discipline, over 20 years, has made me think harder about how I – and we – can understand the power of money, and learn to use it wisely.'

Alison Swinfen is a member of the Iona Community living and working with refugees and asylum seekers in Glasgow. She is Co-convener of Glasgow Refugee, Asylum and Migration Network (as Alison Phipps) and Professor of Languages and Intercultural Studies at the University of Glasgow.

Reinhild Traitler worked with the World Council of Churches, and as Director of the Protestant Lay Academy Boldern/Zurich. Engaged in interfaith dialogue she serves as President of the Interreligious Conference of European Women Theologians (IKETH) and is a member of the Interreligious ThinkTank Switzerland. She is a member of the Iona Community.

Zam Walker lives in Greenock where she is a URC minister, job-sharing ministry and parenting with David, and mother to Taliesin and Melangell. She enjoys discussions, good food, stunning scenery and longs to live in a world where all can enjoy these things fairly and freely. Particularly involved in issues of body theology, especially relating to well-being and travelling with cancer.

Iain Whyte: member of the Iona Community, Church of Scotland minister and former Head of Christian Aid Scotland and Chaplain to St Andrews and Edinburgh Universities. Currently involved in African and refugee issues, research and writing on anti-slavery.

Isabel Whyte: member of the Iona Community, Church of Scotland minister and former Healthcare Chaplain. Engaged in peacemaking and mediation.

Elizabeth Wild is an Anglican priest in North Cornwall with a passionate belief that all people are equally valuable, regardless of the ways that society defines them. In her previous work as a psychologist, she has been privileged to work with people of all ages and abilities in a wide range of situations. She has been a member of the Iona Community since 2000.

The Wild Goose Resource Group is a semi-autonomous project of the Iona Community. It consists of three resource workers: John Bell, Graham Maule and Jo Love. The WGRG exists to enable and equip congregations and clergy in the shaping and creation of new forms of relevant, participative worship: http://wgrg.co.uk/

Jim Wilkie: Arising from his experience of meeting and working with Christians involved in revolutionary situations in several parts of the world, Jim Wilkie prays the Lord's Prayer 'in solidarity with' Jesus, the saints, fellow Christians worldwide, and all who cry to God today. Jim is a member of the Iona Community.

Brian Woodcock: 'I am a URC minister, busily retired in Bristol, and have been an Iona Community member for forty years. Forty years! These days I find that I have known all but the tiniest proportion of those we hold in prayer every thirty-first day of the month. I still feel a personal connection with them. As I do with Key House, that most magical and caring of retreat houses. Such places, such people, have not completely gone. They live in me, enriching my present life. My reflections in this book come from the heart.'

Wild Goose Publications is part of the Iona Community ...

- An ecumenical movement of men and women from different walks of life and different traditions in the Christian church
- Committed to the gospel of Jesus Christ, and to following where that leads, even into the unknown
- Engaged together, and with people of goodwill across the world, in acting, reflecting and praying for justice, peace and the integrity of creation
- Convinced that the inclusive community we seek must be embodied in the community we practise

Together with our staff, we are responsible for:
- Our islands residential centres of Iona Abbey, the MacLeod Centre on Iona, and Camas Adventure Centre on the Ross of Mull

and in Glasgow:
- The administration of the Community
- Our work with young people
- Our publishing house, Wild Goose Publications
- Our association in the revitalising of worship with the Wild Goose Resource Group

The Iona Community was founded in Glasgow in 1938 by George MacLeod, minister, visionary and prophetic witness for peace, in the context of the poverty and despair of the Depression. Its original task of rebuilding the monastic ruins of Iona Abbey became a sign of hopeful rebuilding of community in Scotland and beyond. Today, we are about 250 Members, mostly in Britain, and 1500 Associate Members, with 1400 Friends worldwide. Together and apart, 'we follow the light we have, and pray for more light'.

For information on the Iona Community contact:
The Iona Community, Fourth Floor, Savoy House, 140 Sauchiehall Street,
Glasgow G2 3DH, UK. Phone: 0141 332 6343
e-mail: admin@iona.org.uk; web: www.iona.org.uk

For enquiries about visiting Iona, please contact:
Iona Abbey, Isle of Iona, Argyll PA76 6SN, UK. Phone: 01681 700404
e-mail: ionacomm@iona.org.uk